First-Time Investor's Guide to Real Estate: Pathway to Financial Freedom

A First-Time Investor's Guide to Building Financial Freedom Through Real Estate Investment Properties

Dan Nathan

Paperback ISBN: 978-1-7635285-3-6

Hardcover ISBN: 978-1-7635285-4-3

Website: turbostackers.com

Table of Contents

Introduction

Do you dream about achieving the personal ideal of financial freedom? The freedom that allows you to live your life on your terms without constantly having to stress about bills and piling up debt? If the answer is yes, then real estate investing is the key to unlocking your financial potential.

Real estate has been viewed as a stable and profitable investment opportunity for people who are willing to take practical and calculated risks. This book will explore the importance of real estate investment as your key to financial success and how it can help you attain your personal goals. Sit back, grab a cup of green tea, and explore the world of real estate investing!

Before we unpack real estate investment, we need to get a proper grasp of financial freedom.

What is financial freedom?

Financial freedom is the capacity to live your life without having to stress or be anxious about financial matters. It means having adequate wealth and financial resources to pay for all your expenses without overly relying on your paycheck. Financial freedom allows you to pursue your passions and aspirations and be able to take risks. Financial freedom allows you to make personal choices about the things that you truly value.

For some people, financial freedom entails retiring early and seeing the world. For other people, it could mean starting your own business endeavor on a full-time basis. Financial freedom can mean various things for people, but one thing is clear: You need to plan carefully, make smart investments, and have the courage to take calculated risks.

Attaining financial freedom is a challenging task. It requires patience, dedication, and great amounts of discipline, but with perseverance comes immense reward. Taking charge of your finances by investing in real estate can help you create passive revenue streams that will help you open the pathway towards financial stability.

Real Estate: The Key to Financial Freedom

Real estate is widely viewed as one of the best ways for you to attain financial freedom. It is different from other asset classes, as real estate provides people with a tangible asset that will generate revenue streams that will appreciate over a period of time.

One of the principal reasons why real estate is an effective investment tool is because it offers several channels for generating returns on your investment. People can earn income from rent, selling properties for a profit, or by using property to gain access to credit so that they can finance other investment opportunities.

Additionally, real estate investing has proven to be more stable than stocks, which are prone to market gyrations and volatility. This stability makes real estate a lucrative and attractive investment choice for people looking for long-term wealth-building options.

Another benefit of investing in real estate are the tax advantages that are associated with it. People who invest in real estate are eligible for tax deductions such as:

- property taxes
- mortgage interest payments
- depreciation expenses, which reduce your tax obligations

Real estate investment has been shown to be a dependable way to generate long-term financial prosperity, and with careful planning, you can transform your investment in real estate into a steady revenue stream that will last you well into your retirement.

These are some of the different real estate investment types:

- residential real estate
- commercial real estate
- industrial real estate
- retail investments
- mixed-use developments

You will need to make sure that you choose a real estate investment type that aligns with your financial goals.

What are the benefits of investing in real estate?

Real estate investments are a prudent decision to make for your financial stability. There are many benefits to investing in real estate, such as steady passive income and appreciation of property value over a period of time.

One of the significant advantages of real estate is the potential for a steady flow of income. Rental properties will generate monthly cash flow, which will provide you with a regular source of income that can help supplement your paycheck or even replace it totally. More so, rental rates can be increased over time, which will allow you to increase your profits at a gradual pace.

Investing in real estate means that the value of your property will increase due to inflation and other market considerations. Consequently, real estate investors who hold onto their properties for prolonged periods will see their investments increase dramatically.

Real estate investors have more control and influence over their financial futures because they are in a direct ownership position rather than relying on stock markets and other funds that usually oscillate in value.

Investing in real estate can be the key to unlocking your financial wealth. Whether you are looking for a passive stream of income or creating wealth over a period of time, there are varying types of investments that can help you achieve your financial goals.

By investing in property, you will have the potential to generate regular returns on your investment as you build equity and have cash flow that can be used on other ventures, even expanding your property and wealth portfolio. Admittedly, like any other investment opportunity, there are risks that come with investing in real estate, but if you collaborate with experienced professionals and do your own homework before you commit yourself, you can mitigate these risks and make prudent choices that will set you up for financial prosperity.

The First-Time Investor's Guide to Real Estate is your entry route towards financial freedom. With so many opportunities available to you in this business avenue, this is your chance to begin building a prosperous future for yourself through smart investments.

Let us give you the key to unlocking this corridor of financial stability and success.

Are you ready to change your fortunes? Let's invest!

Chapter 1:

Navigating Your First Investment

Your first investment is an exciting time. You are starting a new journey that will allow you to learn and grow in new ways. On top of that, you are putting yourself in a position where you can increase your income and reach your financial goals.

Understanding the Basics of Real Estate

Before you embark on this journey it is important to understand some of the basic real estate terms. This way you have the knowledge to go through this book with confidence.

Equity

This is the portion of the property that is actually owned by you. While you may "own" the house, the mortgage lender has a vested interest in the property until the property is fully paid off.

The formula that is used to calculate a home's equity is:

Subtract your outstanding balance from the current value of the property. Your equity stake will increase as you reduce your loan amount or when the value of the property increases.

Mortgage

A mortgage is an agreement that exists between the person who borrows money to purchase a property and a lender who has the right to the borrower's property should the borrower default on their loan repayments within the agreed-upon period.

Return on Investment (ROI)

Return on investment is a metric that is used by investors in any asset to calculate and compare how a particular investment is performing. ROI is a percentage that shows your net profit from what you initially put in when you invested in an asset class for the first time.

The return on investment on real estate is generated from appreciation or rental income.

When it comes to the appreciation of real estate, ROI is calculated when you dispose of the property. It is the profit that you get after deducting the property's initial purchase price plus any other costs, such as repairs and renovations, that took place when you still had ownership of the property.

Return on investment formula:

(Sale price of your real estate investment minus cost of investment divided by cost of investment).

If you purchase a property for **<u>$300,000</u>** and sell it for ***$375,000*** after 10 years, the property would have appreciated by **<u>$75,000.</u>**

If you had spent $20,000 on property renovations, the total amount you would have spent on the property would have been $320,000. If you deduct $320,000 from the selling price of

$375,000, your net profit would be $55,000. Divide the $55,000 net profit by $320,000, and your ROI will be 17%.

Capital Gains on Real Estate

If your property is in the US, then when you sell the property for more than what you initially paid when you purchased it, you will likely have to pay capital gains tax on the net profit that has been realized.

What are capital gains in simple terms?

Capital gains tax is levied on the profit that you make when you sell or dispose of a capital asset like a property.

Let us say that you bought a house for $250,000 and then sold it for $300,000. The $50,000 net profit will attract capital gains tax.

Leverage

Leverage refers to the amount of debt financing on a property relative to the current market value of the property. Leverage uses money that is borrowed (debt) to increase the potential profit of a particular investment. When you invest in real estate, the common way to leverage your real estate investment is by using your money or through mortgage financing. Leverage is beneficial when the value of real estate increases, but it can also be disadvantageous if the value of the property declines for whatever reason.

Homeowner's Insurance

When you buy a property, it is also necessary to get homeowner's insurance to cover any losses or damages that might take place, such as fire, theft, or any natural disasters.

The insurance also protects the owner of the property from any liability that might occur through accidents in the home or within the precincts of the property, and your insurance payments are normally included in the mortgage repayments that you are obliged to make on a monthly basis.

Now that we have covered some of the basic terms that are associated with real estate, the next sections will look at the different types of real estate investments that are available to first-time investors.

The Different Types of Real Estate Investments

Real estate investments fall into two categories: physical real estate investments such as land, residential, and commercial properties, and investing in real estate investment trusts (REITs) or crowdfunding channels, which do not require you to own any physical property.

Physical property normally offers higher returns but also requires higher amounts of money up-front and can also have higher maintenance expenses. REITs and crowdfunding initiatives have fewer barriers to entry because you can invest in various types of real estate at a much lower cost when compared to traditional property.

Real Estate Investment Trusts (REITs)

These are the companies that own commercial real estate such as offices, malls, and hotels. You can invest in these companies by purchasing shares on the various stock exchange platforms. When you are investing in REITs, you are investing in the real estate that is owned by these business entities, which carries fewer risks than when you own property directly.

REITs are required to return 90% of their taxable income to shareholders as dividends annually. This then means that investors can expect to receive lucrative dividends on top of diversifying their investment portfolios in the real estate environment. This is a more liquid way to invest in real estate. If you need some money for any reason, you can sell your shares on the stock exchange and have access to what you need.

Crowdfunding

Crowdfunding platforms give you access to real estate investments that you might otherwise not have. Some of the real estate crowdfunding platforms are only available to accredited investors, which are investors that have a net worth value of more than $1 million. Some crowdfunding platforms, such as RealtyMogul and Fundrise, allow non-accredited investors access to various real estate investments that they would not normally be allowed to invest in.

Some of these real estate investments are non-traded REITs or REITs that are not traded on the stock exchange. This means that they will have lower liquidity levels, which means your money will be invested for several years, and there is a chance that you might not be able to take your money out should you ever need it. Crowdfunding platforms are new kids on the block when it comes to real estate investing and have not yet shown that they can weather an economic meltdown so it is good to be cautious when considering this as an investment option.

Residential real estate

Residential real estate are the houses that people stay in, such as single homes, vacation homes, condos, etc. People who invest in residential real estate generate returns by collecting rent from the tenants that reside inside the property. Returns will also be generated from the appreciation value of the property, and investing in real estate can take various forms, such as renting a vacant room in the house or flipping the house in order to generate a profit.

Commercial real estate

Commercial real estate is the area of land that is rented or leased by business entities such as:

- Office space that is used by businesses
- Gas stations
- Shopping malls
- Restaurants and many other business ventures

Unless the businesses involved own the property where they conduct their business affairs, each business is required to pay rent to the person(s) that actually owns the property.

Industrial and retail estates can also fall under this commercial real estate category. Industrial real estate refers to properties that are intended for the production or housing of products, such as warehouses and factories.

Retail space is where a product or service is sold or rendered, such as a clothing store or a business that fixes electronic devices. Commercial real estate usually has longer-term leases and can have a higher rental income than residential real estate, which may translate into steady and long-term rental income for the investor who owns the property.

Raw land

Investors in the real estate space usually buy tracts of land for commercial or industrial development purposes. However, when you buy land, you will need to conduct thorough market research, especially if you have intentions of developing the property yourself.

Investing in raw land is more tailored towards investors who have a fair amount of start-up capital to invest, and you must also have deep insights on real estate concepts such as:

- building codes
- zoning laws and regulations
- flood plains and other hazards
- deep understanding of the residential and commercial landscape

When you are considering investing in real estate, such as residential and commercial properties, you have to conduct intensive research, which does not involve a down payment. You have to have valuable insights on the local market, and when there is no interest or appetite for commercial or residential properties in your vicinity or when the prices of real estate are declining, you might find investing in such circumstances burdensome and a drain on your finances.

If you prefer to play a more passive "silent investor" style role, REITs and crowdfunding platforms are the best bet to add real estate to your investment portfolio without actually owning any tangible property.

Now that you have a deeper awareness of the various types of real estate investments that are available to you, we shall now turn our focus on the basic principles of real estate.

The Basic Principles of Real Estate Economics

The attributes of the real estate market

Real estate is different from the other asset classes, as they are defined by economic, financial, and legal terminology. The real estate environment forms part of the regional and national economic architecture, and if there are any changes in the economy, these will inevitably influence the real estate landscape.

The unpreventable risks in the real estate market

The real estate markets are constantly adjusting to a balance; property prices are altered according to fluctuations in demand and supply and are also impacted by changes in the local and national economic environment.

These intricate attributes make investing in real estate risky, and this risk is aggravated by the sizeable capital costs that come with it. These property transactions will also require legal authorization and recognition that come with the rights of property occupation.

The legal rights, and the ability to trade and transfer those rights, ownership, and possession make real estate uniquely different from other assets (Clifford, 2017).

The real estate market is also subject to the risks that are associated with the market, financial risks, and various other business risks that are involved.

Property evaluation

As a potential investor in real estate, you need to conduct an assessment of the property, which entails calculating a prediction of some of the price cues that you can see from market forces, financial considerations, accounting factors, economic conditions, and the prevailing laws that guide the real estate landscape.

Real estate evaluations are the force that drives the real estate market, and this process of real estate assessment is also referred to as real estate appraisals.

Let us take a dive into the principles that affect real estate valuations. The value of real estate is affected by particular economic principles, and these include:

Economic Principles of Anticipation

Investors in the property space purchase properties with the intention of generating future benefits. This precept states that the value of real estate rises using the anticipated rewards and benefits, which can take the form of monetary benefits or other amenities that will be realized from a property in the future.

For example, you buy a home that has a sizeable swimming pool for $200,000. A similar property that lacks a pool sells for $130,000. Effectively, you are paying $70,000 for the anticipated benefits that come with the pool, not the actual cost.

The Principle of Supply and Demand

The rarity of a commodity influences the value that it has by generating a greater demand for the particular asset. As an example, when the supply of properties that are facing the sea becomes less prevalent, the value of these properties goes up to be able to meet the demand for them. The principle of demand is also influenced by desire; if there is an abundance of apartments in a particular area, the demand for them will decline. This would mean that the values of real estate and rental income will inevitably go down.

The Principle of Substitution

The value of real estate is usually set at the cost of a similar property that is a desirable substitute.

In theory, no one should pay more for a property than what it would cost to obtain a site by purchase and sale and to construct a building of equal appeal and utility (Clifford, 2017).

Balance Principle

This principle talks about the relationship between the costs, additional costs, and the value that it returns for the property. For every dollar that you invest, the value of the property needs to rise by more than the dollar that you initially put in.

The Economic Principle of Progression

The central idea surrounding this particular principle is that the price of a property rises with the value of the surrounding location. For example, if you are selling your house and the properties in the surrounding neighborhood have been recently renovated, this will increase their value, and the price of your own real estate will increase due to being in this particular location.

The Principle of Progression

This is the inverse of the progression principle above. The price of your property will decrease because of the value of its site. For example, even if you have a beautiful house that has been renovated but your area has been negatively affected by a natural disaster, then regardless of the beauty of your home, its value will decrease due to this catastrophe.

Are you ready to know more about the trends and dynamics that influence the real estate market? Read further.

Navigating the Real Estate Market

Do you know how much the forecasted value of global real estate will be by the year 2030?

The global real estate market is forecast to reach USD $9,756,804.10 million by 2030, with a compound annual growth rate (CAGR) of 4.14% from 2023 to 2030.

How has the COVID-19 pandemic affected the real estate market?

The pandemic has accelerated trends like remote work, digital transactions, and flexible spaces within the real estate market.

Identifying the Emerging Markets in the Real Estate Environment

The attraction of the emerging markets in the real estate environment is underpinned by their anticipated growth, diversification, and being viewed as lucrative investments.

As cities around the world transform and demographics shift, new markets rapidly rise, which offers a conducive environment for real estate investing.

How can an investor identify emerging markets?

These are some of the strategies that you can use:

- **Market research**. Intensive market research will help you identify regions that have real estate opportunities that can yield growth and steady returns.

- **Economic indicators**. You have to look at the following factors:

    - Job opportunities that are available in a particular city.

    - The rate of population growth.

    - The infrastructural development that is taking place can hint at an emerging real estate market.

- **Real estate trends**. Digging into real estate trends, such as the prices of real estate and rental income dynamics.

How can you leverage emerging markets?

- Strategic and careful planning
- Establishing networks and strategic alliances
- Utilization of technology
    - Using modern technological solutions to keep track of market trends, manage your own investments, and enhance your decision-making as to where you might need to invest.

Emerging markets present a slew of opportunities for people seeking to invest in the real estate market. However, you must be willing to undertake strenuous market research, make shrewd assessments, and take prudent action. By deepening their understanding of the subtle differences between emerging markets, potential investors can place themselves in a position to leverage real estate possibilities. This will cultivate financial growth and diversify your investment portfolio as well.

Mitigating Risks in Real Estate

Can there be a foolproof investment? All investments carry their own risk factors, and so is true with real estate investments. Investing in real estate carries a lot of risk, but there are plenty of ways in which you can mitigate and avoid major consequences.

If you proactively take steps to lessen risk, real estate investing can be significantly less risky than investing in other asset classes. Let us look at how you can avoid the usual pitfalls that are associated with real estate investing.

There are different types of risks in real estate:

Representative Risk

These are the intrinsic risks that are associated with investing in a particular asset class. For example, let us say you invest in construction projects, which carries the risk of you not making any money until the project has been completed. There are risks as they relate to delays on site, adverse weather conditions, budgetary constraints, and approval risks that need to be factored in.

Credit and Replacement Risk in Real Estate Investments

This type of risk is associated with old buildings. As the older buildings fade and new buildings are constructed around them, investors must make the decision to replace the old buildings due to the competition of the newer buildings.

Commercial real estate can attract a credit risk as companies of a reputable stature and credit profile can go out of business. So, while the net profits in commercial real estate are high, you must also take into account the risk that they can potentially bring.

Market Risk

Changes in the real estate environment, whether favorable or unpopular, occur frequently, which makes managing risk a crucial aspect of investing in real estate. When you have a comprehensive risk strategy, you can identify and quantify risks to make sure that you make sound investment choices. Prudent real estate investing requires an investor to possess the necessary knowledge and comprehension of present and historical market trends in order to determine what can influence market changes.

Conduct your research on property

Do your market research in several locations. You may find that some locations are riskier than others, so by having a deeper understanding of the real estate environment in various cities, you can potentially augment your profits and avoid risks.

Portfolio Diversification

You can mitigate your risk and increase your profits by investing in particular locations. However, this does not mean that you should invest all your money in one basket. For example, if all your properties are in a locality that is prone to natural disasters or unpredictable market shifts, your entire investment portfolio can be liquidated at once. You should explore different cities and other areas so that you can make sensible investments that can generate steady returns.

Bias Towards Residential Real Estate

No matter what the state of the market is, people will always require shelter to live in. By focusing your investment efforts on the residential property space, you will increase your chances of generating returns.

Get good insurance.

This is a foregone conclusion. You want to get insurance because there are things that can happen that are beyond your control. You may need to consider opting for an insurance scheme that covers everything so you are prepared should there be unforeseen eventualities.

You have been introduced to the basic terms and concepts in the real estate environment. The next step involves choosing the right property that is in line with your goals.

Chapter 2:

Finding the Right Property

When thinking about property investment, one of the first things that may come to mind is investing in an apartment or a house. While this is real estate or property investing, it is not the only type out there. There are many different types of real estate investments and it's important to understand what they are so that you can make an informed investment decision.

Analyzing Property Types

In this section, we are going to go through the different property types out there. There are pros and cons to each type and the one that's going to be best for you will depend on your ultimate goals and how much money you have to start with. Eventually, you could invest in multiple different types of real estate to diversify your real estate investment portfolio, but you don't need to feel pressured to do that right now.

Residential

Residential real estate is one of the most popular types of real estate investments. This is because it is one of the safest types of real estate investments, plus it is likely to be the most accessible for a beginner or first-time investor. On top of that, real estate is always in demand. People always need a place to live so it is easier to put strategies in place that can assist you with making a good residential real estate investment so you can profit from it.

There are many different types of residential properties out there. These could be large single-family homes, apartments, multifamily homes, townhouses, and condominiums. Basically, any kind of property where people live. When you invest in residential property, there are many different ways and strategies you could use to make money from this. You could purchase the property at a low price, fix it up, and then sell it for a higher price to make a profit in a short period. You could also purchase a property and rent it out either on a short-term or a long-term basis and make money through rental income. Another option is to play the long game and collect a profit through appreciation value. This means that you purchase a property, live in it, and when you are ready you can sell the property for a profit. Suppose you have done your due diligence and picked the right property and are taking care of it. In that case, property appreciation will work in tandem with any other type of residential property investing strategy. This means that you could earn a profit from selling any residential property you have regardless of the income strategy you have used for it.

Commercial

For those with access to more funds, commercial real estate can be a good option. There are many different types of properties that can fall under the category of commercial real estate. The main purpose of commercial real estate is for business purposes. Some examples of commercial property are office spaces, retail, hotels, and hospitality spaces. When a property in this category is purchased, income generation is the main goal. This means the investor will need to do a lot of research in order to make a viable investment.

Commercial property is also heavily impacted by what is going on in the economy. For example, an investor purchases commercial property in the retail space. They decide to open a shopping center. If there is an economic downturn and people do not have a lot of spare money to spend, then the stores in the shopping center will start to lose money. This means they will no longer be able to pay their rent and will need to give up their businesses. This will impact your revenue and you will likely start losing money. Only once the economy picks up again will you be able to recuperate. Another example is when the COVID-19 pandemic hit and everyone started working from home. Many commercial property owners suffered financially because businesses did not need the office space any longer.

When done right, a commercial property can make a large profit. With this comes a large financial risk. This is why it is important to take the time to conduct research before making such an investment. Many commercial real estate investors get into partnerships with other investors so that there are more funds available and the risk is split between all involved. There are many factors that need to be considered before making a commercial real estate investment. One of the most important things is the market demand. You need to know that there is a demand for this type of property in the area you are looking to invest in. It isn't going to be a good idea to invest in an office building in a rural area or farming town. There will be very few businesses that need offices in those types of areas. You would also need to know the types of tenants you are trying to reach and what their needs are.

Industrial

This type of property is for manufacturing, distribution, and warehouses used for storage. You will usually find these types of properties on the outskirts of a city since they are large and can be loud, release steam/gases, and are usually not easy on the eye. These types of property users will have specific needs, so it is important to know what the target market is like. The area you invest in needs to be one with industrial possibilities and needs. This type of property investment also comes with a lot of risk and you will need a good amount of capital to get started. Having market experience and knowledge is essential to ensure that you make a good investment. It will be difficult to use this type of property for anything other than what it was intended for.

Land

There are different types of land that will fall under this category. Land can be a good investment because it is a finite resource. We cannot make or create more land. Raw, infill, and subdivided land are all categories of land that can be invested in. Raw land is land that has basically been untouched and it can be used to build upon. Subdivided land is land that has already been divided into smaller plots. Often this is done for residential lots. Someone might own a large area of land and will have it divided for individual investors to purchase for their own uses. Infill land is land that is currently underutilized and can be developed into something else.

When buying land, it is important to know the area and what that land can be used for. This will help you identify whether it will be a good investment. There are many ways to make a profit from this type of investment. The easiest way is to simply purchase the land and sit on it until the value goes up. For example, purchasing a piece of subdivided land and then waiting for the other properties to be developed. Once the area is up and running and people are moving in, your land will be desired by those who want to build their own houses on it. You could also purchase land and build something on it yourself. Then you can rent it out for a profit. Research is important so you can be sure you are purchasing a property in a good location that will be able to bring in profit when the time is right. In most cases, you will need some time to pass before you are able to make a profit from land investment.

Assessing Property Value

When it comes to assessing a property value there are many aspects to consider. It is not just about the actual property you are purchasing. Real estate investment takes time and careful evaluation before you decide to make a purchase. Doing the research and knowing what to look out for will ensure that you make a good profit from your investment.

Conducting a comparative market analysis (CMA) is going to help you understand how much a potential property is worth and whether or not it's going to be a good investment. When doing a CMA, there are various factors that need to be considered. They will either add to or take away from the overall property value. When you are making a real estate purchase, you should look at the factors that would increase the property value so that you can be sure you are making a good investment. Many first-time property investors simply buy the cheapest property only to realize that it's very difficult to sell later on or to even rent out. This is not a position you want to find yourself in because you want to make sure you are making a profit as soon as possible.

In general, a comparative market analysis helps you to see the price of the current property you own, and how it's going to do on the market, as well as how to price your property. When you are making an investment, you can still use the same principles of market analysis when purchasing a property. This way you are also aware of how much you will need to spend for the type of property you want. It will also help you to identify an overpriced property so that you are not wasting your money.

You can get a CMA done for you by a real estate agent or a broker. This will be a professional CMA that will allow you to fully understand how much you could potentially sell your current property for. When the analysis is done, the aspects that will be looked at include the neighborhood details about the property and comparable aspects to other similar properties. After this is done, the real estate agent or the broker will adjust for any differences and then determine the price per square foot of the property. Because there are a lot of calculations involved and a lot of information that you might not readily have access to, getting a professional to do a CMA for you is likely the best way to move forward.

That being said, knowing what factors influence the value of a property will help you to make a better financial investment when the time comes for you to purchase a property. It will also result in you getting a better score in a CMA when you are going to sell that property later on down the line. You should be considering these important factors way before you decide to make a property investment.

Location

The first factor that is important to consider is location. You will hear many real estate, investors spout *location, location, location.* This is because it is likely one of the most influential aspects when it comes to the value of your property. When people look for a place to stay or a new home, the first thing they do is look at the location. They will want a place that is close to amenities, has a low crime rate, good infrastructure, and is in an area that is aesthetically pleasing. You will find homes that are almost identical, but one would go for twice the price just because of the location. This is why property prices in big cities near economic hubs tend to be so much more expensive than properties in rural areas. Location is also important to consider because it is one of the things that cannot be changed once you purchase the property. You should always make sure that you do your research on the location you are buying in to make sure that it is one that people want to stay in.

Many different aspects indicate a good location. For one you want to make sure that the property is as central as possible so that it is easy to get around. Whether you are looking to live in the house, rent it out on a long-term basis, or do short-term rentals, the people who live in the house must be able to get around and find things they need easily. A central location will have shopping malls, child-friendly areas, restaurants, and stores quite close to it.

A property in a location that is developing and being built up is a really good sign because it means there is investment in that area. Even if the properties are not worth a lot at this moment, it is a good indication that they will be in the future because there are more amenities being built in the area. If you drive around the area and you see a lot of development and building happening then you know this is a good sign and property values are likely to increase in that area.

Another aspect of location that is important to consider is where the actual property is located in terms of other amenities and aspects. Even within a good area, there are some locations that can bring property prices down. For example, a property that is close to a busy road or highway tends to be lower value because it is inconvenient for the person living in the home. Highways can be incredibly loud and can also feel quite unsafe since there is a lot of traffic in that area. Another example would be an apartment that is right next to a bar or club. While this is technically close to amenities it is not really a good location because there is going to be a lot of noise in the area which will be inconvenient for those living there. On the flip side, certain amenities could increase the value of property such as a property near a lake. Lakes and large bodies of water that are well cared for are peaceful and a huge drawcard for people which means the property will be more valuable.

Condition of the Property

Once you have the location sorted out, you also have to consider the condition of the property as well as the overall size. Properties that are in better condition do have more value however, depending on the type of investment you are making it might not play that big a role. If you are looking to purchase a property very cheap so that you can flip it and sell it for a profit, then it might not matter that the condition of the property is not the best. With this being said, whenever you are making a property investment, you must fully understand what needs to be done to the property before making the purchase. This way you can budget for the renovations and not be constantly surprised as you are fixing up the property.

The size of the property also depends on the goals you have as a property investor. If you are planning to purchase a property for yourself to live in, then you will consider your own needs but if you are looking to rent out the property either long-term or short-term, it is important to understand the needs of the people that will be staying in your property. This way you can choose a size that is going to be the most attractive to your ideal renter.

Market Conditions

Market conditions are another important aspect to consider because this will dictate the current buying and selling prices of property. Sometimes the market is good and you will be able to increase your property value but other times the market is bad and even a stunning property in an amazing location is not going to be able to sell for as much as you might have hoped. These market conditions are influenced by things like employment rates, economic conditions, and interest rates.

Community and Neighborhood

Another important thing to consider is the overall community and neighborhood in which your property is situated. If the location has a good reputation, then the properties within that location will have more value. Even if you are not looking to invest in a family-sized home, good schools and a safe area will always be an indication of a good area. It is also a good idea to look at the recreational facilities, and how easy it is to access public services and transportation.

Finding the right property to invest in does take a lot of research but it is worth it. You will never regret taking some extra time to make sure you are choosing the right property so you are able to make a sound investment. The next step in the process is to start considering finances. Real estate is an expensive investment, so knowing how to finance your ideal property is essential. In the next chapter, we will be diving deeper into this important topic.

Chapter 3:

Financing Your First Investment Property

Understanding how to finance your investment property is incredibly important. The world of real estate investment financing can seem complicated. Since investing in real estate does come with a larger price tag than most purchases, it is important to make sound financial decisions so that you aren't wasting your money and getting into unnecessary amounts of debt that are difficult for you to handle. Managing your current finances well and starting investing with a stable plan, will result in you being able to get the most out of your investments.

Exploring Financing Options

There are many different financing options when it comes to real estate investment, but the most common is a mortgage. This is a loan that allows you to purchase and maintain a house, land, or any other type of real estate. With a mortgage, the property you purchase acts as collateral if you are unable to pay back the loan. This means that the lender will be able to repossess the property if you do not honor the payments that you have agreed to. As the person who takes out the mortgage, you are agreeing to pay back the lender through a series of regular payments over a specified amount of time. An interest rate is agreed upon and is added to the principal amount that you have borrowed. Mortgages tend to have lower interest rates than other types of loans which makes it a more manageable and beneficial way to fund purchasing property.

Since purchasing a property is incredibly expensive, most people do not have access to that kind of money up-front. Taking out a mortgage allows someone interested in purchasing real estate to access the funds and pay it back over time. Once the mortgage is completely paid off, then you will fully own the property and it will be free and clear. Mortgages are long-term loans and typically run somewhere between 15 to 30 years. You can pay off your mortgage quicker if you have access to the funds to do so. This will reduce the amount of interest you will be paying over time. However, it is not necessary to do this, if it does not align with your finances and the goals you have set for yourself in this regard.

Many different service providers offer mortgages so it is a good idea to compare rates so that you can get the best deal. Banks and other financial service providers are where you will look for a mortgage. Have a look at the terms of the loan, as well as the interest rate. You can apply for many different mortgages at the same time. Typically, the lenders will have a look at your credit score and decide how much they are willing to lend you, and at what interest rate. The better your credit score, the higher your chances of getting a good interest rate and good terms for your mortgage. If you haven't started working on your credit score yet then it is a good idea to start as soon as possible. This will benefit you in the long run. Once you have all the pre-approvals and the proposed mortgage from the lenders, you can compare each one and choose the one that's going to benefit you the most. There are different types of mortgages including fixed term, straight mortgages, adjustable-rate mortgages, reverse mortgages, and interest-only loans.

Even though a mortgage is the most popular way to finance property it is not the only way. Accessing a private money loan could be a good option if you are trying to avoid all the red tape that is involved when it comes to getting the mortgage. There are different terms with a private money loan because you are going to access this loan through a private lender. You might be able to access the money quicker, but the interest rates and payment terms are discussed between the borrower and the lender. You also need to find a private lender who is willing to move forward with a deal like this. You will need to offer up some collateral to take a loan like this. The collateral could be another asset to own like a separate property.

Managing Investment-Related Expenses

When investing in property, it is important to understand that there are up-front costs as well as ongoing costs that must be considered. Creating a realistic budget is going to help you see how much you will need from the get-go. This will allow you to plan and also ensure that you're not spending money unnecessarily. You'll be able to see exactly what is necessary and what you should be cutting back on so that you can use your money efficiently, leading to a maximum amount of profit.

When thinking about how much property investing is going to cost you, one of the easiest things to understand is the up-front cost of purchasing the property. You will know the amount when you purchase the property and there is little to no guesswork involved. You will also be able to only look for properties that actually fit within your budget and how much you can afford. Other things to think about would be the cost of renovation and other up-front expenses. Think about things like property rates, body corporate levies, and utilities. On top of that, you want to think about things like how much is going to cost you to furnish the apartment or home if you are looking to rent it out.

Let's talk about a few of the expenses that are not as clear-cut as a property investor might first think. Firstly, we have registration fees, which are the fees that are applicable when purchasing a property. This fee ranges from 2% to 4% off the total value of the property. There are also broker fees if you have used a real estate agent to help with the property purchasing process. You will need to make sure you understand the percentage of commission that comes with engaging with a real estate agent, as this does vary from agent to agent. It is prudent to expect around a 2% to 7% commission on the overall price of the property you are purchasing. Closing costs are another thing to consider. These are the fees that need to be paid to close a deal when it comes to a real estate transaction. Since there is a lot of paperwork involved when purchasing a property, these fees cover that. Then we have maintenance charges, especially if the property you are purchasing is in a gated community or some other type of community. This fee is imposed to have funds to upkeep common areas such as parks. When purchasing in a specific area, it is important to ask about the maintenance charges so you are fully aware of how much you will need to budget for it.

Once you have all of this information, you can start creating a budget so you are aware of how much you will actually be paying throughout the process. Know how much you can afford and start breaking down the different costs so that it fits within your budget. When purchasing a property there are going to be some areas where the costs are one-off or due in a lump sum, and other costs that are due every month or over different pay periods. For example, a fee if you have used a real estate agent is a one-off thing once you have purchased your property. However, maintenance fees and your mortgage payments are things that you will need to pay every month. You can create a monthly budget to highlight how much you should expect to pay each month and see how it can work into your personal budget. Then you can also create an overall spreadsheet of how much the property is going to cost you and highlight the one-off fees that need to be paid so that you can be sure that you have enough money set aside for these things.

When you are managing real estate and making it an investment opportunity, it is so important that you manage the cash flow. You essentially have a business at this point. Especially if you are using your property to rent out and bring in an immediate income. Cash flow ensures that you are bringing in enough money to cover all expenses so that you are not forced to take out money from your personal budget or take out loans to cover the expenses. In order to ensure that you have enough cash to put into the various areas of your real estate investment opportunity you need to make sure that you are aware of how much everything is going to cost you. Then you will need to manage these expenses. In some cases, there are going to be fixed expenses that you can't do much about, but there will also be expenses that you can cut back on to increase your cash flow and ensure that you have enough money to put into other areas. Looking into how you can reduce your utilities and maintenance can go a long way. You don't want to cut corners but you also don't want to spend more than necessary. Understand your expenses and make sure that they fit within a realistic budget so that they can be covered within the amount you are making from your investment.

You will also need to ensure that you are making your debt repayment on time so that your credit score remains positive. Managing debt becomes an incredibly important part of real estate investing and managing cash flow. Ensure that it is a priority and that you always have enough money set aside just in case you do not make an income from your investment. You will need some additional cash saved for a rainy day so that you can cover all expenses and ensure that you do not default on payments. Keeping track of your income and your expenses is essential so that you know exactly what your money is doing and how to manage it well. This will also allow you to do your best to match up the income and expenses columns of your budget so that you are not going overboard in your spending and can maximize your profit.

Preparing for the Financial Aspects of Investing

Preparing your finances for real estate investing should happen as early on as possible. It shouldn't be something that you only think about when you are ready to purchase your first property. Setting yourself up for success will allow you to have what you need in order to invest without wasting time.

One of the first things that you want to work on is your credit score as this is a cornerstone to getting a mortgage with good interest rates and loan terms. If you have a poor credit score, then you are likely to not get a mortgage. If you are granted a mortgage, it might not be for the amount you need or might be at a much higher interest rate that will cost you in the long run. Typically, a good credit score is around 670 to 739. Slightly lower is still okay but you start creeping into dangerous territory the lower you go. Anything over 800 is classified as an exceptional score and you could probably get amazing interest rates and access to loans and mortgages. It is important to try and get your credit score as high as possible.

There are quite a few different things that come into play when your credit score is calculated. This includes how long you've had your credit, how much credit you have, whether or not you have defaulted or are under debt review, and how many different types of loans or credit you have. If you want to build up a good credit score, you first have to start with having some credit. Opening up a credit card is one of the easiest ways to build your credit since it is accessible to almost everyone over the age of 18. Once you have a credit card, you must use it properly. Rather than using it as additional money you get to spend, use it as a tool to build your credit score. You will need to use money from your credit card to build your credit score but this doesn't mean that you have to spend unnecessarily. For example, you could budget a certain amount for grocery shopping, but use your credit card to purchase your grocery items. At the end of the month, you can transfer the amount you have budgeted from your salary into your credit card so that your credit card is not gaining interest and putting you in debt. At the end of the day, it is really important that you don't buy things that you cannot afford.

Looking at the other criteria for building good credit, you need to make sure that you don't default on any payments and make it a priority to pay your bills before they are due. All of your bills will have a deadline, and if you do not pay them on time, this is going to reflect negatively on your credit score. If all of your bills are due on different dates in a month, it can be difficult to keep track, so you can phone the various companies and ask if you can change the payment date to suit you so it's easier to just pay everything at once. You could also set up an automatic payment for all of your bills so you don't even have to think about it or worry about it.

It is also important that you review your credit report every so often so that you are aware of what is going on with it. If you notice something is amiss, then you can handle it immediately so that it doesn't continue to create a negative situation with your credit score. You can check your credit report for free from various credit unions, including Experian and Equifax. You also want to ensure that you are paying off any debt that you currently have. Try not to take on any other unnecessary debt that you cannot afford. If you have a debt payoff plan, this is going to help you stay committed to paying off your debt and ensure that you do not let it take over your life. With every debt that you currently owe, it is best to pay at least the minimum so that you do not default on any of the payments. Then you can start focusing on paying more than the minimum on your debt so that you can pay off quicker and ensure that you're not stuck in a debt cycle.

The Loan Process

Once you've done your best to ensure that your finances are in good standing, you will then start moving into a space where you can apply for a mortgage or a home loan. This might not be right now if you are working on your credit score and other financial aspects but it's important to understand the process so you're not caught off guard when the time does come.

The first thing you are going to need to do is do your research so that you are aware of which financial service providers do offer mortgages and then compare what they offer so you can narrow down which lenders you would prefer to use. You will need to fill out a loan application with your chosen financial service providers. In these applications, you will need to fill in details about all the assets that you own, your income and debt, and any other financial information they might request from you. You will also need to provide them with documentation to support the application. Using this information, the provider will be able to decide how much you can afford and the type of loan that's going to work best for your situation.

Once that is done, you will get a preapproval letter if you have met the basic standards. Preapproval is your go-ahead to start looking for a property, because it means that you are likely to get the mortgage for the specified amount that is in the preapproval letter. It also helps when you are searching for a property to purchase, because you can show the sellers that you will have access to the funds to make the purchase. Once you have found the property that you want to purchase, you can make an offer based on the preapproval and the amount stated.

You do not need to offer the maximum given to you by the lenders so make sure that you do negotiate an offer that is going to work best for you and your financial standing.

If the deal goes through and the sellers accept your offer, then you'll need to move on to the rest of the loan process. Remember that preapprovals will only last for two to three months, so if you have not found a property at this stage, you will need to reapply for preapproval. In some cases, an inspection and appraisal of the property you want to purchase will need to take place before the loan is finalized. This is where everything is put out on the table, including any other loans on the property from the previous sellers so that everything is cleared before you can continue with your transaction. You will need to provide the lender with as much supporting documentation from your finances and other areas. Try and get this information to them as quickly as possible so that there aren't any holdups. At this point, a loan processor will ensure that everything is verified and accurate and then the final underwriting process will start so that the loan can be approved or denied. If it is approved, then you can go ahead and sign it and you will be able to purchase your property. It might take three to five business days for the funds to clear and be at your disposal. Once this happens, the journey of becoming a property owner begins.

It might seem like the biggest hurdle in the real estate investment market is the finances, but there are many other things that need to be considered. Ensuring that you can do an effective real estate market analysis means that you will be able to choose the right properties that will bring in the most amount of profit. This is an incredibly important aspect of real estate investing. In the next chapter, we will be diving deeper into this subject.

Chapter 4:

Real Estate Market Analysis Made Simple

Conducting effective market analysis is what is going to help you make the best choice when it comes to your real estate investment. It is tempting to simply jump in or follow the advice that you find online or through your friends, but it is imperative that you take the time to do your market analysis. This way you can make sound investment decisions that you are confident in.

Fundamentals of Market Analysis

There are many different things that come into play when analyzing the market. The reason you do a market analysis is to understand the market better so that you are able to make more well-rounded financial decisions. There are a variety of components that come into play when you are doing a market analysis. Each of these things affects the price of the property both currently, and in the future. On top of that, you can also find out whether the area you are planning to purchase in will be in demand or not. The goal of doing a market analysis is so you can collect relevant information to make the best decision about either acquiring, selling or renting a property.

Real estate agents and other real estate professionals conduct market analysis so that they can fully understand what is going on in the market. You can conduct your own form of market analysis so that you are aware before you buy or sell property. Typically a comparative market analysis is done by comparing different properties in the same area and which have the same attributes to determine a fair price for the property, either to buy or sell it. If you are looking to buy or sell property, then you might also look into doing a comparative market analysis. What you have to do is look at the property you are currently interested in buying or selling, and then compare it to other properties in the same area with the same attributes. So if you are looking to buy a three-bedroom home in a specific area, you would then look at other three-bedroom homes in that area and see how much people are selling for. This way you can decide whether you are getting a good price or not. Remember that you'll have to look at various criteria in order to get an accurate comparative market analysis. Make sure that the properties you are comparing are as similar as possible so that your analysis is accurate.

As mentioned above, there are many things that need to be considered when doing a market analysis. For example, you will need to look at employment patterns and demographic trends. If the area you're looking to invest in is growing in terms of population, this is a good sign. People looking to move into the area means that there are probably developments and economic benefits to doing so. The property prices will likely increase as more people move in and more investment is made into that area. However, if people are moving out of the area, it is a good idea to figure out why as this might not be the best investment if properties in this area might start to decrease in value. Other things to look at are amenities, infrastructure, crime levels, new development and construction, and overall occupancy rates and prices.

When you are doing a market analysis, you will need to get your data from somewhere. The good news is that there are lots of places where you can access information to help you do this analysis. For example, you can go onto property listing websites such as Zillow and you can do a comparative analysis based on what you find. Almost every aspect of the homes listed will be there, so you have free access to all of this information. If you are looking for information in the neighborhood or area, then you can do a quick Google search to see what is around the property you are planning on selling or buying.

Evaluating Market Trends

As time goes on, you may notice trends in the real estate market. It is important to understand these trends, so you know what to expect, and can plan and prepare. Certain trends make certain types of property more valuable and others less valuable. Keeping your finger on the pulse will always be the best way to stay on top of any market trends. If you subscribe to real estate investment blogs, or YouTube channels, then you'll get the information firsthand. It is a good idea to see what other property investors are doing so that you can gauge where the trends are moving. Social media can also be a good indicator, although not necessarily as accurate. Having a look at the type of style of property that is popular on social media can give you a good indication of what people are looking for right now. Talking to other property investors can also give you a good indication of what is going on in the property market.

Currently, there are many different trends popping up due to the current state of the world and the economy. For example, because of the rise of remote work, people are looking for homes and properties that have dedicated office spaces so that people are able to work from home. Even people who have office jobs might want an office space for part-time work or perhaps they have a hybrid work environment. Since all of these things have become more popular, having an extra room in the house for dedicated office space has become more important. We are also living in the age where sustainability is really important so investing in sustainable buildings and properties can really be a big attraction. Another big shift in the real estate market is the integration of technology and smart homes. If you are looking to rent out your property or even sell it, it might be a good idea to integrate smart technology to bump up the price and generate more interest in your property.

It's not just what is going on in the actual property that can affect the prices and the general market, but also external factors. The economy and economic shifts have a huge impact on real estate. For example, when there is an economic downturn or a recession, it means that people are not willing to pay large amounts of money for property since they do not have that money to spare. In a time where layoffs and retrenchment are constant, people might be looking to move to cheaper areas or cheaper properties, or even downsizing, in order to alleviate some of the financial burden. There might be policy changes on a governmental level that could impact the property market.

Something else to look into is any technological advances that might make it easier or harder for you to get a property on the market. For example, since people are always online, it might be a good idea to do a virtual walk-through of the property on social media, or the property website, as this could easily attract more buyers since they are able to see what they are investing in before they even come and visit the property. This could be a good way to increase the overall value of the property since you are making your property more available to people who are not in the area, and therefore increasing the demand.

It is also a good idea to understand how long you are willing to take on the investment as this can impact whether an investment decision is going to be good or bad for you. When you are doing your analysis, there might be indications that show you that in the long term, the investment could be a good idea even though it might go through a rough patch right now. Or perhaps the opposite is true: investing now is good for a short-term investment but not a long-term one. Short-term investments allow you to invest in a quick return on your investment so that you can make your money back in a shorter amount of time. If you do your research well, then a short-term investment could be a lower-risk investment since less time passes and you can be sure that the analysis and research you have done will still be relevant. Long-term investment might be a higher risk since you may not always know what the future holds, but when we look at the property market, values do increase over time so this is a pretty safe strategy. However, you do have to bear in mind that you will need to hold your investment for a long time in order to make an income or reap the rewards of your investment. Long-term investment is also a long-term commitment which means that you have to be willing to stick with your investment and put in the work over time. You might not be as flexible with your investments, and they will not be liquid. This means you will likely only be able to access the funds later on, especially if you are holding a property and not renting it out. Thinking about the type of real estate investment you want to make will impact how you look at the market trends and whether or not they are going to work in your favor.

Local vs. National Market Dynamics

When doing a market analysis, it is important to understand that there is a big difference between local and national market dynamics. This is going to heavily impact many different areas, so what might be happening on a national level does not necessarily reflect on a local level. For example, on a national level there might be a decline in property prices due to economics or another factor. However, on a local level, in a specific area, the property prices might be increasing, and there might be more demand for property in that area. This means that, even though in a state or a country there could be a specific real estate trend, this might not be the case on a more local level in a specific neighborhood.

It could also be true that on a national level, there could be a positive trend in property, prices, and demand, but this is not the same on a more local level. If nationally the property prices are increasing, it is not a good idea to assume that this will also be taking place at local levels. A neighborhood could be experiencing a decline due to low employment rates or specific government policies that are only applicable to that area, and other local factors. Perhaps the quality of the schools in the district is going down or public amenities are not being taken care of. Maybe there is a higher crime rate than normal, and the area is in general on a decline. It doesn't matter if all the national trends are positive because if there are negative aspects in the local property market it is not going to be a good investment for you.

This is why it is so important to do your analysis and research on different levels. You'll need to understand what is going on on a national level so you can get a good overview of what to expect. Then you want to move your analysis into more specific areas so you can get a better idea of the local market dynamics. You never want to invest in property in a specific area if you have not done an analysis or evaluation of that area. You will also need to figure out exactly why the local market dynamics are different from the ones on a national level. This is regardless of whether the market dynamics are moving in a positive direction or a negative one.

It is also important to understand that trends tend to ebb and flow both on the national level and on a local level. There are exceptions to the rule, but it is important to understand the ebbs and flows of the markets so that you can also accurately predict what is going to happen in the future. Your analysis should not just be based on what is happening right now, but what happened in the past so you can get a better idea of the timeline and the trends that do take place. Even if there is a negative market trend taking place right now, you might see that after this negative trend, there is possibly going to be a positive one to balance it out, and therefore it might be an optimal time to invest when the property prices are low, because you can be sure that the property prices will increase shortly.

Real estate investing is all about balancing the risk and reward. Even with the best analysis, there's always going to be some risk involved when it comes to investing in property. This is not said to discourage you, but rather to make you aware that you will need to put in the word to ensure that you are protecting yourself while you are investing in real estate. Even though real estate tends to be quite a stable investment, you must recognize that it can go up and down. Diversifying your real estate portfolio is probably one of the best ways to protect yourself. However, this might not be completely realistic at the beginning, since real estate tends to be quite an expensive investment. Having a long-term plan for your real estate investment is going to assist you with creating a robust investment portfolio and investment plan.

Along with your investment plan, you will need to know the legal and tax aspects that come with investing in real estate. This is often not something thought of when you first start investing in property but it's definitely something that needs to be considered. This could make or break your real estate investment journey and that is why it is so important. In the next chapter, we are going to be diving more into these essential topics, so that you can be fully prepared.

Chapter 5:

Legal and Tax Essentials That You Must Know

When you are looking to invest in property, it is very important that you understand the legal and tax aspects to make sure that you are complying. Even though it might seem tedious to go through this process and make sure that everything is in order, not doing so has consequences. Making sure that everything is in order right from the beginning means that you will not have to stress out or worry in the future and you can concentrate on actually investing in property and making money from that. Note that any legal and tax information given here applies to the US only; not all countries have capital gains tax, and tax deductions for landlords are not always available elsewhere.

Understanding Real Estate Law Basics

When it comes to property law, it is important to understand that different rules and regulations are in place for different countries, different states, and even different areas. This is why this can be such a complicated topic to cover. Before you decide to invest in property in a specific area, it is imperative that you fully understand the property laws and regulations so that you can go into the process with your eyes wide open. Some areas are a lot stricter when it comes to the rules and regulations and others are not so much. It is not good to assume that the rules and regulations in one area will be the same in the next.

You can easily find information about local property laws online and on the local government websites. This will be the most up-to-date form of information so you can be sure that you are complying. Even if you have been in an area for a long time, it is also important for you to continuously stay up-to-date with the local laws and policies because these can change from time to time. As a property investor, it is your job to be in the know when it comes to laws, rules, and regulations. Not fully complying with these means that you might be liable for fines and fees. Some of these are really expensive and can make a huge dent in your overall profits when you are investing in property. It is best to avoid this completely by ensuring that you are staying abreast of all the new policies and laws. You can also hire a lawyer to assist you with this process as they will notify you when there are changes or anything that you need to be aware of. It does take some of the burden off you and you can be sure that you are getting accurate and current information. Not only that, but a property lawyer will be able to assist you with developing strategies to ensure that you are not paying more than you need to while still complying with any policies and laws that have been put in place. Be aware that these lawyers do come at a cost so you will need to work it into your overall investment budget.

When you are buying or selling a property, there are legal steps that are involved and it is good to be aware of these. Buying a property is not just about making an offer and signing a contract. There are actually quite a few steps that need to be done. Let's do a quick walk-through of the entire process so that you know what to expect when you purchase your first property. Remember that this process is going to take place over a few weeks and is not something that happens quickly. The timeline can change based on various circumstances so it is important to have a realistic time frame in place when you begin. Let's say you have found the perfect property you want to invest in and it is at a great price. You and the person selling the property have come to an agreement and everything is looking good. From here, you would want to open an escrow account since there are still quite a few steps that need to be completed before the property can be moved over to your name and you can pay the seller. An escrow account is basically like getting a third party involved to hold the documents and money until everything has been settled in the process. Once all the formalities have been taken care of, the money is moved to the relevant parties so that the transaction is secure. This is for the benefit of the buyer and the seller so it is important to do this.

Next, you will need to do a title search and check insurance to make sure that when you are buying the property there is nobody else that can claim it. It is just confirmation that the current seller has legal rights over the property and has the authority to transfer it over into your name. You will also need to hire an attorney to make sure that everything is in order, and that you are following the steps correctly. Once all the legal aspects have been taken care of, you will need to negotiate the closing costs with the seller. There are more financial aspects than simply purchasing the property—closing costs will include things like the home inspection and pest inspection, which needs to be done to make sure that the property is actually worth what you're paying for it. Once the closing costs have been agreed on, you can go ahead and get a home and pest inspection done for the property. Based on the results of these inspections, you can then make a decision as to whether you want to continue with the purchase or back out completely. In some cases, you will be able to negotiate with the person who is selling the property for them to pay for pest control or any damages that were not disclosed earlier in the process. It is essential that you do these inspections because there can be a lot that is hidden away and it can cost you down the line.

Based on the outcome of the inspections and legal processes, you will get the opportunity to renegotiate your offer. Remember that your offer is not set in stone and is based on everything going according to plan. If something is found that is going to cost you more than expected then it is important to renegotiate the offer to include necessary repairs and pest control. How you choose to renegotiate is going to be completely up to you, but make sure that it is realistic and will cover any additional costs that you might face.

Once the negotiations have concluded, and all parties are happy, it is important that you look at your interest rate as soon as possible. The interest rates that are offered for mortgages can be volatile which means that you need to make sure that you look for a good interest rate for your loan as early as you can. This way you don't have to stress out about market fluctuations and you can be sure that your interest rate will stay the same and is at a good rate. The next step is to consider the contingencies. When you make your offer, it should be contingent on being able to obtain financing at a good interest rate, the inspections giving a positive result, the person selling the property being honest about any issues, results from the pest inspection, and any agreed-upon repairs being completed. These will be removed by set dates when you make the offer to make sure that the conditions are met for your offer.

Once all of this has been completed and both parties are happy, you need to do a final walk-through before you sign the closing papers. The purpose of this walk-through is to make sure that everything looks exactly as you want it and that there were no additional damages caused through any repairs or inspections since the last time you visited the property. You will also have the opportunity to verify that any agreed-upon improvements or fixes have been resolved. On top of that, you want to ensure that everything that has been included in the agreement is still there and has not been removed. For example, if the purchase agreement states that the barbecue stand will stay with the property, you will need to make sure that the barbecue stand is still there and has not been removed. If it has then you will need to raise this and make sure that areas of the agreement have been fulfilled. Once this is done, you can get the paperwork signed, but make sure that you actually understand the paperwork. If there are any legal terms that you are unsure of, ask your lawyer to assist you. From here the transfer of the property into your possession will begin.

Tax Implications of Real Estate Investing

Taxes are a really important topic when it comes to real estate investing. Many people have quite a negative view of taxes, but when it comes to investing in real estate, there are tax benefits that you can take advantage of. This helps to lower your overall tax so that you are paying less taxes overall. When you own real estate in the US, you have to pay property taxes and capital gains taxes. Property taxes are the taxes that are imposed on you by your government to help pay for community projects and services. If you have a mortgage, then it forms part of your mortgage payment and is based on the value of your home and the land it is built on. The thing to take note of is that you will continue to pay property taxes, even after your mortgage has been completely paid off. For as long as the properties are in your possession, you will be liable for property tax. It is important to make sure that your property is correctly assessed so that you will not be taxed more than necessary. Most people do not do this and can end up paying over 50% more on their property taxes than what is required. You can also lower your property tax if you are a senior, veteran, or spouse of a veteran, disabled, or have a property on agricultural land.

Capital gains tax is tax that you will pay on your property as an investment. If you sell your property and make a profit from it, then you'll be liable for capital gains tax. This type of tax is only applied to the profit that you make through selling your property and not the overall worth of the property. If you did not make any profit from the sale of the property, then you will not need to pay capital gains tax. If you use your property as a way to make an income through renting it out, then any income you make from that will also be taxed, but this will be taxed as ordinary income.

You want to work on paying as little tax as possible legally. There are many ways that you can reduce your taxable income by legal means so that you are not overpaying in any area. It is a good idea to get a tax consultant or accountant on your team to assist you with this as it can save you a ton of money. As you bring in more properties into your real estate investment portfolio it becomes even more necessary to have this professional on your team. They will know exactly how to handle taxes so that you will save as much as possible. There are many deductions that you can access as a property owner in order to lower your tax liability. Some of these are your mortgage interest, insurance, property taxes, operating expenses, and maintenance and repairs. If you spend money in any of these areas, then this can be deducted from your overall taxes and this means that it will lower the amount of tax you pay.

Legal Aspects of Financing and Mortgages

When you are financing a property and taking out a mortgage, there will be quite a few contracts and documents that you will need to read through and sign. While it might be tempting to simply just sign everything without reading through it, this is a bad idea. Remember that your mortgage or any other property financing option is a long-term commitment so it is important to understand what you are signing up for so that you are happy with the terms.

The two major contracts that you will be signing are called the mortgage note and the security instrument. In the mortgage note, you will have all the details on how you are expected to pay back the mortgage. It will list how much you have been loaned, as well as the down payment, interest rate, and the length of the loan, as well as any other important information. The security instrument is a much longer contract and has a lot of legal terms within it. This document spells out what will happen if you do not hold up your end of the bargain. Let's say for some reason you are unable to make your mortgage payments. Then the security instrument will detail what will be expected and what will be the process moving forward. It basically outlines the terms of owning the property and under which terms the lender can take back the property from you. You will have to follow all the terms within this document in order to keep possession of the property until you have paid off the mortgage. This document will also outline exactly what you are allowed to do with the property and what is prohibited.

When it comes to other financing options for your property, legal and financial aspects will come into play. For example, you might want to modify your current loan, which means that you will change the original terms of it. If you want to extend the loan or reduce the interest rate then you can contact the lender and inquire about modifying your current loan. With this option, the lender does not have any obligation to accept your request or to renegotiate the loan. This means that modifying a loan can be quite difficult and it is completely up to the lender to decide whether they want to allow you to do it or not. With this being said, it is always worth it to find out if they are willing to modify the loan if you are struggling or you just want better terms on your loan.

The other option would be refinancing your mortgage, which means you are taking out a new loan and replacing your existing loan. Doing this allows you to change the terms of your current loan since you have a brand new one. You don't even have to stick with the current lender. If you choose a new lender, they will pay off your current loan, and then you'll enter into a new contract with them. This is typically a lot easier and is why people choose to refinance rather than modify their loans. It is important to ensure that you have done your research if you are looking to refinance because you want to get better terms than what you currently have.

Chapter 6:

Risk Management

Just as with any other investment, real estate investment is a risk. Even with the best information and robust research, there will always be a risk that you will lose the money that you have invested or your investment will not turn out the way you planned. Investors don't like to think of risk when they are investing, but it is best to be prepared so that you can manage any risks and reduce the impact of unfortunate circumstances.

Understanding Investment Risks

There are various types of risk that are tied to real estate investing. Understanding these risks will allow you to analyze the different areas and come up with a strategy that's going to serve you best. The goal is to limit the amount of risk that you are going to take when you are investing. There is no need to take unnecessary risks. Otherwise, you will end up losing out or continuously stressing yourself out.

The biggest risk that you take when investing in real estate is the general market risk and this is something that you cannot control. General market risk includes things like a recession, economic downturns, inflation, deflation, increased interest rates, and anything that will cause investment sectors to increase in volatility. The best way to protect yourself from risk is to do your research and diversify your investment portfolio. You don't want all your money to be in one type of investment, otherwise you are putting yourself at an even bigger risk. Then you have financial risk which is tied to the amount of debt that you are getting yourself into in order to purchase real estate. If you are taking out a loan that you cannot pay back or that is causing you to be financially unstable, then even something really small will have a big impact on your finances. It is important for you to ensure that you will be able to pay for your investment even if you do not make returns or a profit immediately.

In terms of the property that you have purchased, there will also be a risk involved there. For example, you might want to take a risk on a property in an up-and-coming area because it is cheaper and there is some indication that the area is being built up. This might be a smart move, but there is a risk involved because you are not 100% sure whether this will pan out or not. Another example of a risk that is specific to the property purchased will be based on the type of property that you have invested in. Single-tenant properties tend to be quite secure since people are always looking for places to live. This is especially so if it is in a good area with competitive rent. Short-term rentals or holiday rentals could end up making you more money, but there is a higher risk involved because there is a higher turnover rate, which means there's more work involved and more risk that your property will not be booked out all the time. Remember that you cannot avoid all risks—you just have to make sure that you are able to handle the risks you do decide to take.

When you are an investor, you must be able to take on some amount of risk because this is just part of the game. This goes for investing in real estate and other types of investing as well. Investors who have a higher risk tolerance are more willing to invest in things that other people might not readily jump into. The fact of the matter is that more risk does bring the opportunity for more reward. It also brings the opportunity for more losses. In your investment journey, you will definitely have to make some risky moves if you want to grow your investment portfolio to be the best that it can be. As a first-time investor, you shouldn't focus on taking the biggest risks, because you don't have a lot of capital to play with. Your first few investments should be focused on understanding the real estate market so that you have more knowledge to base your risky decisions on later. You can make a few risky decisions if you want to, but ensure that you have the mental fortitude and the finances available so that it doesn't completely wipe you out if the investment goes bad. You should never make a risky investment by putting all of your eggs in that basket because it can cause you to lose everything. This is why it is so important to think of risk as an opportunity, but be smart about the way you handle it.

While there is definitely risk in all types of investment, real estate is unique. Real estate assets are not very liquid. This means that you can't sell and liquidate your investments quickly if you see things are going bad in the market or in another risk category. With something like stock investing it is very easy to sell off all your stocks if you see the market is plummeting. This means that you won't lose as much as you would if you had held onto those stocks. However, when it comes to real estate, it takes time to sell your property so having a long-term mindset is best when investing in this manner. You don't want to invest any money that you're going to need in the near future and you definitely don't want all of your cash to be tied up in your real estate investments. Real estate should form a part of your investment portfolio, but not all of it since there are so many restrictions on how you can access the money from this investment. Having additional funds in other investments and in cash means that you aren't going to be strapped if there is a financial emergency or you need access to money. You can allow your real estate investments to continue to grow over time so you can see the best results from it.

Risk Mitigation Strategies

We have already spoken about how diversifying your real estate investment portfolio can help you with managing risk. This is definitely one of the best strategies to mitigate risk in any kind of investment, but it is important to know what diversifying actually is. When you diversify your investment portfolio, it's not just about buying a whole bunch of properties so that you have a bigger investment portfolio. Diversification requires intentional work and research so that you do it properly. For example, if you are looking to invest in commercial real estate you might decide that you want to diversify your portfolio so you invest in more spaces and other properties that fall under this category. Let's say you did this before 2020. Then the COVID-19 pandemic hit, and everybody was working from home and packing up their office bases because they were no longer in use. This means that even if you try to diversify your portfolio by purchasing more properties, you are still going to lose money. This is not an effective way to diversify because all of your investments are in one category. In fact, this is riskier because now you're going to lose all of your money or at least most of it.

This is why you need to plan properly when you diversify your real estate investment portfolio. You will need to invest in different types of property, different locations, and different real estate sectors in order to have a diversified portfolio. All of your property investments should not be in the same area, the same sector, or of the same type. Using the above example, if you decided to invest in residential real estate on top of commercial real estate before 2020 then when the pandemic hit you might've lost money with your commercial real estate but you still could be making money through your residential real estate. This could've held you over until the pandemic was over and commercial real estate started being used again.

Diversifying safeguards you and ensures that you are protected from any unplanned situations that could harm your investments.

It is also important to remember that diversifying your portfolio and real estate investment, in general, is not about simply purchasing a bunch of different kinds of properties and leaving it at that. You will need to manage your investment portfolios by constantly doing research and staying on top of the trends. This will allow you to figure out the best next move for you so you can decide on other property investments, or perhaps sell some of your current investments so that you have more liquidity to invest in more profitable investments.

Investing in real estate is all about being adaptable because we can't always predict what is going to happen in the future. Being adaptable means that you will always be ready for what lies ahead and you won't get too attached to a certain type of investment or type of strategy. The world looks very different now than it did 50 or 100 years ago. There are new types of investments and much more information out there, so it means that being adaptable to change and being ready for it can help you make the biggest profit. One of the best strategies that you can use for your real estate investments is to have an adaptive pricing strategy. It is common to see people with rental properties set a price and leave it at that. They might believe that the price they set is what their property is worth and are not willing to go lower. Even if you have the most amazing property, people will only be willing to pay a competitive rate based on what is going on in the market. Staying informed about rental and sales data, market trends, and supply and demand will help you price your property in a way that attracts people and reflects the market conditions.

Something that many property owners do not consider as an investment strategy is managing your property correctly. Remember that regardless of the type of property you own, it is an investment. This means you need to take care of it because you never know when you might need to sell or rent it out. A well-maintained property will become an asset and is far less likely to become a liability. If you own a property and do not take care of it and keep up with the maintenance, then it is likely that the value will start to go down. You might think that you only need to take care of the maintenance issues when you want to sell or rent it out but you never know what conditions this will be under. If you need to sell quickly so that you can liquidate your investments, but have not kept abreast with the maintenance it is going to be incredibly difficult for you to get your money's worth out of that investment. On top of that, it is a lot more expensive to take care of maintenance issues if they have been unattended for many years. Sticking to a maintenance schedule where you ensure that things get done every year will be beneficial to your pocket and your investments.

Long-Term Risk Management

Real estate investment is a long-term game and that is why you need to plan to manage risk over a long period of time. You might have done all the necessary research before you purchased or invested in a property but this process is always going to continue. Doing ongoing marketing analysis means that you will always stay informed about the transaction changes that could potentially impact your investment and then you can create a plan that can mitigate the risk as early on as possible. It is a good idea to surround yourself with information about the real estate market so that you will have easy access to the information as soon as it is released. Subscribing to newsletters, YouTube channels, and even social media pages that are dedicated to real estate investors does help. While not all of the information might be relevant, it is good to surround yourself with real estate information so that you are immersed in that world and if something piques your interest or seems relevant to you, you can do some additional research.

We spoke about contingencies in the contract process of taking out a mortgage for a property. It is important to make sure that any contingencies are planned for before you rent or sell your property so that you don't run into any problems in your investment journey. This means taking care of your property, ensuring that you are advertising it correctly, and disclosing relevant information to the potential buyer. This way, the process is smooth and you can ensure that you will get the most out of your property.

Any kind of long-term risk management strategy means that you will need to build some resilience and learn from your failures as well as your successes. While you might not want to believe that there will be some failures in your investment journey, it is pretty much inevitable. If you speak to any real estate investor or any type of investor, you quickly realize that all of them have hit a rough patch or made some mistakes that resulted in outcomes that were not ideal. This is simply part of life and learning how to get back up when you are knocked down is going to be a vital skill. It will allow you to keep going and not get discouraged if something were to happen. This is not to say that you have to fail and make mistakes, but rather be prepared if it does happen.

In fact, learning from your mistakes is one of the best ways to learn because it solidifies the information and allows you to learn on the go. If you make a mistake and have to face the repercussions for it, it is highly unlikely that you will continue making the same mistake. Mistakes actually help make you better so if you ever do fail, look at it as an opportunity to learn rather than actually being a failure. It is important to analyze why you failed or made a mistake so that you know exactly what to do to avoid it in the future. This way you can change your strategy to fit the new information that you have learned to ensure that your overall risk management is getting better. This will improve your decision-making in the future. The more you invest, and the longer you are in the investment game, the easier it is going to be to understand the process and the better decisions you will make for your investments. Unfortunately, there is no shortcut when it comes to this, so it is definitely best to take things as they come and be willing to continuously learn and implement new strategies as you grow as a property investor.

Chapter 7:

Building Your Real Estate Network

When you invest in real estate, it is easy to think that you should be doing it on your own since it is going to be your money that you are investing. However, this is definitely not the case. Building a strong network can help you to gain information, make connections, and even access more funds in order to invest more effectively. A strong network is so valuable when you are an investor.

Importance of Networking in Real Estate

Working on developing a strong network has a direct impact on how successful you will be as a real estate investor. This is because your network will allow you to access opportunities that you wouldn't be able to on your own. On top of that, other people will share knowledge and insights on things like the market and regulations. It can be difficult to stay on top of all of that information on your own, so having people who are connected and who have the same interest in real estate as you means that you can expand and grow your knowledge in the many different areas of real estate investing.

It doesn't matter which type of real estate investing you are looking into doing because a network can assist you with all of them. When you have a strong network, it means that people trust you and have a relationship with you so you will be the first person they consider if they are looking to buy or sell a property. This means you will get prime opportunities and the best buying or selling rates. You also have access to knowledge which is incredibly valuable as a new investor. While making mistakes is inevitable, if you have a strong network, the number of mistakes you will make will severely decline. You have people who have been in your shoes before and who can advise you on the best steps forward. They will share their knowledge and experience. You can use this information to better your decision-making and ensure that you are putting your best foot forward when it comes to your real estate investment.

Another important aspect of having a network is that it will build trust within the real estate community. If you know the right people, they will connect you to other people who have experience and opportunities for you. Being connected to the right people means that your reputation improves and other people will more readily trust you and want to work with you. It makes it so much easier to buy and sell properties when people believe that you are trustworthy and they want to work with you.

Networking can feel intimidating, especially as a beginner, and if you don't know anybody in the real estate game. Taking those first steps to network will be the best thing that you can do for your real estate investment career. The first thing you want to do is identify key networking opportunities around you. You need to figure out where other people are going to be and make your way there. Look for events where real estate professionals can connect. There are tons of real estate conventions and events. You just need to know where they are and sign up for them. It's a good idea to search the internet and even social media to find these events. Connecting with real estate-specific social media pages is a great way to stay connected with other real estate professionals and many organizations have social media pages and will post about networking events. Look out for conferences, seminars, and other local meet-ups. If there aren't any in your area, you can take the first step by creating your own networking event. Have a conversation with a few real estate agents and other real estate professionals and see if you can gain some traction and create your own event. Real estate agents are great people to know because they have connections with real estate developers, investors, and other real estate professionals and they are easy to get a hold of and know who they are.

Connecting With Professionals and Mentors

Connecting with the right real estate professionals and mentors can really help you to increase your knowledge and become a better investor. Attending networking events is one of the best ways to find a mentor and other professionals to connect with. A mentor will help you in all areas of your investment journey. They will be somebody you can go to and ask for help, guidance, and support when you need it. This will need to be somebody who has been a real estate investor for a longer time than you, and has more experience, and therefore more knowledge to share. It can be daunting to ask somebody to be your mentor, but the truth is that many professionals would love the opportunity to share the information they have gained with somebody else. You don't have to approach people and actually ask them to be your mentor, but you can ask them if they are willing to share their knowledge and help you. The goal is to connect with people who have more experience than you, so that you are able to access knowledge and opportunities through them.

There are also paid mentorship programs that you can access online. All it takes is a quick Google search to find a few of these. If you do go this route, it is important that you do your research and ensure that the mentor is somebody who can be trusted. Check out reviews and news articles on the mentorship program you are signing up for. Another way to access professionals and mentors is through online real estate forums and using your existing network to find people. You might not think that you have a network at this point but if you know people then you do. Ask around and see if any of your friends or family know people who are real estate investors. They may be able to connect you to them and you can start a relationship from there.

While you are on the journey of looking for mentors and professionals you can be proactive and access information through podcasts and books. The great thing about podcasts and books is that you can access a mentor and people with more experience than you without actually connecting with the people. These resources offer knowledge at a high level and can guide you through the process of real estate investing based on their experiences. There are so many podcasts out there who bring in professional real estate investors, and ask them questions, or allow them to share their story. This is information and knowledge that you would not have access to in any other way, so it's so important to take advantage of it. These podcasters and the authors of the books might also host real estate events, so it is important to follow them on social media platforms so that you are aware of any events they host so you can attend and perhaps meet some professionals in real life.

Another important group of people that is important to connect with is real estate developers. These are the people who are building real estate and selling it. Developments attract a lot of attention, and if you are able to connect with the right developers, it means that you will have a firsthand pick of new developments, and these developers will be able to share market insights and research with you that could be incredibly valuable to your real estate investment journey. You can use the similar tactics of social media and attending networking events to connect with these people. However, sometimes a more direct approach might be the way to go. If you find that you're not getting anywhere with your networking approach, you can call real estate developers and have a conversation with them. There might be a few people who are not willing to talk to you, but you'll be surprised at how many people are willing to have a conversation. That conversation is how you start building your network in the first place, so taking that first step can be so valuable.

Networking Strategies and Etiquette

Knowing how to network is one of the most important things when it comes to this topic. It is all well and good to attend networking events and find people who are in the real estate market, but if you don't know how to network and you don't do it properly, then it's not going to help you in the way you might hope it would. It is important to understand that networking is something you need to do on a continuous basis. It's not just about meeting people and leaving it at that. Putting yourself in a position to meet people is just the first step, because you need to work on building a relationship with them.

You'll need to be brave enough to approach people and speak to them. You can't simply approach people and ask them to be part of your network as this usually does not work. Instead, you should look for opportunities to build a relationship with them and have meaningful conversations. In order to do this, you will need to have knowledge of the real estate market and be somebody who is interesting to get to know. Your network will grow if people like you on a personal level and you have something to offer them. As a new investor, it can seem daunting to talk to people who have been in the real estate market for a much longer time. This is why it is important to read and listen to podcasts so that you are aware of real estate topics that are currently circulating. This way you will have something to add to the conversations and contribute on a full level.

Initiating conversations can seem daunting, but once you get the hang of it, it is something that will become second nature to you. Remember that when you go to networking events, the goal of everyone there is to meet other people. This means that they are going to be willing to have a conversation with you if you introduce yourself to them. All you have to do is walk up to different people with confidence, simply introduce yourself, and ask them about themselves. When people talk about themselves, they immediately feel connected to the person they are talking to. Everybody loves talking about themselves. This is not the time for you to share all of your dark secrets or share why you are the best at what you do. Rather, get to know the other person so that you have a foothold for continuing the conversation. You'll be able to find things you have in common with them, and it will be easier for you to connect with them on a long-term basis. Remember to print out business cards so that you can easily hand out your information. While this might seem like an old-school thing it is still important and relevant today. People put all contacts in their phones these days, but just in case the opportunity doesn't arise to do that you can quickly hand out your business card so that people have your information. It is also important that you get their information so that you can be proactive with your networking.

Once you have made that initial connection, it is important to not let the relationship die. You will need to follow up with them and make sure that you are continuing to build a relationship. This means sending them an email every now and then, giving them a call, or even sending them a message. Since networking is a more professional space, a good way to follow up and continue the connection is to find relevant articles, podcasts, and news stories to send to people. Think about the conversation you had and see if you can build on that when you follow up with them. Remember, people love to connect with people who are going to add value to them.

It is a good idea to put some time in your schedule to maintain your network. You don't want to simply call people when you need them because this can make them feel like you are using them rather than actually trying to connect with them. You don't have to send them a message every day but every few weeks or months it is good to check in with your network and make sure that everybody is still on your side and doing well. The goal is to make people remember you so that if there are opportunities that do arise, you will be somebody they think of first. This is why it is so important to maintain your network and not simply meet people and leave it at that.

It is a good idea to build your social media presence as that makes it a lot easier to connect with other people and to maintain your network. Sending people things over social media is easy and requires very little work. There is a lot of information and tips and tricks on social media so it makes it very easy to continue connecting with people. On top of that, social media allows you to connect with people and grow your network to a place that you wouldn't ordinarily have access to. In order to build your online brand, you will need to be consistent about posting and you'll need to make sure that you are posting relevant content. You can create a separate profile for your real estate journey so that you are not sharing all of your personal life on this profile. However, it is important to make sure that this profile is personable and does show off your personality as well.

One of the most important things to remember when it comes to networking is that you need to be willing to add value to others. While you will be reaching out to people to gain opportunities and information, they will want to build a network that will benefit them as well. This means if they reach out to you for assistance then you need to be willing to help them out. It is so important to be known as somebody willing to assist because this is something that's going to follow you around as you continue with your real estate journey. People are willing to go the extra mile for other people who have done the same for them. This is not the time for you to be selfish, or only concerned about what you are getting out of this relationship. Rather, focus on what you can give to other people as this is going to open up a lot more doors than simply trying to connect with everybody so you can also ask them for help. It is a good idea to check in with the people in your network and see if there's anything that you can do to help them. Sometimes people might not know that you are somebody that they can rely on so taking the first step is a good way to ensure that you are building your reputation in this manner.

Networking is definitely a skill, and it will take time for you to learn how to build it. This is why it is so important to get started as soon as possible so that you can be exposed to various networking situations and build up your skills. While it does seem daunting at first, eventually it will become second nature to you. Remember that there are networking opportunities all around you, and you don't only have to network at dedicated networking events. You can find people wherever you go so it is important to make networking a lifestyle. This means that you are always ready to network and connect with people. This could be in the line at the supermarket or even at the dog groomer. You really never know when you are going to meet people who can assist in your real estate journey, so always be on your toes and be willing to talk to and connect with people.

Networking will become part of your life and something that you will do on a continuous basis, regardless of where you are, and what you are doing. With this being said, you don't want your real estate investment journey to become an obsession to the point where you let your personal life and other areas of your life slip. In the next chapter, we are going to be talking about how you can balance your real estate investing with your personal life so that you do not feel overwhelmed in the process, and that you can still enjoy your personal life throughout this journey.

Chapter 8:

Balancing Real Estate Investing with Personal Life

Finding balance as a real estate investor can be difficult because you want to put your all into the journey. However, it is so important that you find this balance, because you want to make sure that this is something that you can sustain for the long term. One of the biggest mistakes people make is that they do not consider their personal life and then investing in real estate either becomes an obsession or becomes something that is completely unrealistic for them. Working on finding the balance from the beginning can help you build a stable foundation for your investment journey and ensure that you are taking care of yourself and other areas of your life.

Recognizing the Importance of Balance

Being able to create balance in your life, when you are working on investing in real estate is such an important thing. It can be so easy to let your investments and professional pursuits overtake everything in your personal life, but if you do this, it will have many negative effects. As humans, we all need enjoyment in our lives in order to thrive and increase our productivity. People often think that the more they work, the more productive they will be, but this is not necessarily the case. We need to be able to disengage from our work lives in order to enjoy our personal lives and watch that area thrive. There are many facets in life that need to be taken care of and that is why it's so important to find this balance so you can put your time and energy into the right places.

When you first start out investing, you will likely be incredibly motivated to put all of your effort into it. This is a great space to be because it means that you are willing to learn and grow and give it your all. With this being said, it is very easy to end up burnt out if you do not prioritize balance and the other important areas of your life. If you have ever been burnt out before you will know it feels like the world is weighing you down. When you think about work or doing something professionally, it can feel like an uphill battle because your mind, willpower, and your body are not working together to help you with your goals. This is why it is so important to find this balance, so you do not end up at the stage where things become increasingly difficult for you to do.

The goal is to integrate your investment journey into the rest of your life in a way that's still going to allow you to be productive in all other areas while thriving in your investment journey. This is where setting boundaries comes into play. When you set boundaries, you are setting clear indicators of when you should be working and when you should allow yourself to rest and relax. Having these clear boundaries allows you to have a guideline or an outline of what your days should look like so you can honor the variety of needs you have. It also allows you to use your time more effectively so that you can be more productive in a smaller amount of time and don't need to overcompensate in other areas. When you set boundaries, you are allowing yourself to dictate how much time you will be putting towards your investments and how much time you're going to allow yourself to rest, relax, and take care of the other areas of your life. You'll be setting specific hours in the day you will dedicate to your investments and the rest of the hours will be used for other pursuits.

It is also really important that you take breaks within the day and if you feel things are getting too heavy, you must disengage to allow yourself to decompress and come back to normal. When you take these breaks, it is important that you practice self-care by doing things like eating healthy, exercising, and making sure that you are sleeping enough. These three areas are the ones that tend to suffer the most when you bring something new into your life. We tend to give up sleep so that we can work more or choose not to exercise or eat healthy because we want to put in more time and energy into our investment journey or other work pursuits. While this might seem like a good idea in the moment it has many negative effects in the long term. Exercising, eating healthy, and sleeping well are what gives you the energy and the mental fortitude to actually be productive, so if you are not focusing on these areas, the other areas of your life will start to disintegrate and this is not going to be good for your investment or other areas of your life.

On top of being focused on investing in real estate, you also need to realize that investing in yourself is one of the most important investment decisions you'll ever make. When you invest in yourself, you are providing yourself with the knowledge and confidence to make better decisions and be an overall better person. Investing in yourself is one of the only investments that you can never lose. Things could happen to your real estate investments that you have no control over but when you invest in yourself, this is something that's going to stick with you for the rest of your life. It is going to allow you to be more flexible and help you to grab new opportunities as they come. You'll be able to adapt, change, and keep your mind healthy. In order to invest in yourself, you will need to prioritize your own health and self-care, as well as continuously learn and grow in the areas that are important to you. Setting aside time to do this every day is so important.

A big part of investing in yourself and creating balance in your life is being able to set realistic goals that will allow you to excel and grow. Many people do not set goals effectively and that is the reason why they find it very difficult to achieve success. One of the foundational principles for setting goals is called the SMART goal-setting framework. Each letter stands for a specific area that you will focus on as you are setting your goals. These are specific, measurable, attainable, relevant, and time-bound. When you focus on each one of these areas in the acronym, it allows you to focus on goals that are going to serve you best and make sure these goals are achievable. From here, you are able to set steps going forward so that you have a clear plan. Goals are very important, but it is even more important that you have a plan in order to reach them. Ensure that you understand the steps and can do them every day so that you get closer to your goal in incremental movements. These small steps will help you to reach your goals in a way that's healthy and attainable. Remember that a marathon is completed one step at a time.

Time Management and Efficiency

Now that you are adding a brand-new task into your life, it becomes even more important that you manage your time effectively. The other areas of your life will still need to be taken care of and the responsibilities you have are not going to diminish so this means that you will need to use the time that you have in the day to include real estate investment in a way that's not going to make you feel overwhelmed. The best way to do this is through time management techniques. We often hear people saying that they wish they had more time in the day but the truth is that when you're able to use the time you already have effectively, this is not an issue. Time is a finite resource, which means that we only have so much in the day and there's nothing that we can do to increase the amount of time that we have.

One of the most effective ways to utilize your time is through time blocking. This is when you look at the amount of time you have in the day and then block out specific pockets of time for the different tasks that you need to do. You can do this on a calendar or a specific time-blocking app or even do it on a piece of paper. When you time block, you have to decide exactly how much time you need for each task that you have to do in the day. This means that the first step is exactly what you need to get done throughout the day. Create a list for yourself of all the different tasks that you need to get done and then next to each task highlight how much time you need for them. This gives you a realistic idea of how much you can actually get done within the day. You can look at your week and start scheduling tasks into relevant timeslots so that you can ensure that everything is getting the right amount of time and attention. Remember to be realistic when you are time-blocking. People overestimate how much they can get done in a small amount of time which leads them to feel completely overwhelmed with the amount of work they need to do. It is best to understand what your capabilities are so you can set realistic time blocks to get your work done efficiently and help to feel more productive.

Remember that managing your time is not just about the time when you are working or investing. You will also need to carry over time management techniques into the rest of your day. Your morning routine is one of the most important things you can work on if you want to be more productive throughout the day. How we set up our morning helps us to physically and mentally prepare ourselves to be productive throughout the day. This doesn't mean that you have to do work early in the morning but rather do things that are going to help you be better. You can start by doing something hard so that you put yourself in the right frame of mind. This is why many people choose to go to the gym in the morning because it checks physical exercise off the list as well as doing something challenging. On top of that, exercising in the morning allows you to have more energy throughout the day and feel better about yourself. You could also do things like reading, journaling, and planning out your day.

Using technology to your advantage can also help you to schedule your day and ensure that you are not overcommitting. The app Calendly allows people to book appointments with you in the time slots that you have allocated for it. This takes the work out of scheduling things manually and it also allows you to see your calendar right in front of you so you are aware of what you need to do. Other forms of technology and apps that are really useful to a real estate investor are things like e-signature documents, virtual reality, and data analytics and market insight apps and technology. All of these things can form an important part of investing in real estate and help you to automate areas so that you are not spending your time doing things that something else can do for you.

When you are working on managing your time effectively, decide which tasks are important for you to do and which tasks you can delegate to other people or technology. You might feel like you are the only one with the right experience or knowledge to do all the tasks in your daily calendar. This is simply not true. When you delegate tasks, it allows you to free up time to do things that are actually important so you are not wasting time and stressing yourself out with things that other people can do. In order to delegate effectively you'll need to figure out exactly what your important activities are. These will be the things that generate the most value for your business. You don't want to delegate tasks to the point where you are giving up the responsibility to other people, as this is not effective either. Write out a list of all the important tasks that only you can do such as networking creating the right strategies, closing the deals, and negotiating. Once you have this list you know that everything else that needs to get done in the day can possibly be delegated to somebody else or to a piece of technology.

When you delegate you don't want to simply give your tasks to any random person. The goal is to delegate to people who are competent enough to do the tasks effectively and ensure that you are reaching the results you want to. This might mean that you have to bring people on board and pay them for their services so that you know you are getting the best quality. You might need to hire an assistant to help schedule your day and take care of admin tasks. Perhaps you want to hire somebody to take care of your website or social media so that you don't have to be the one who is actively posting and thinking about content. Perhaps you will need to hire somebody to take photographs of your investments and your property. You might also want to hire a real estate agent to do the bulk of the research for you, so you don't have to spend time doing this. There are so many resources and professionals out there that you can bring onto your team to ensure that you are reaching maximum productivity, but also allowing you to manage your time so that your personal life does not suffer.

Maintaining a Healthy Lifestyle

Being able to maintain a healthy lifestyle is one of the best things that you can do for yourself and your real estate investment business. This is such an underrated piece of advice, but is something that needs to have more light shone on it. Managing real estate can be stressful and it does take up a lot of your time. That is why you have to be the one to put your foot down and ensure that you are maintaining a healthy lifestyle so you can be around for a long time to enjoy the fruits of your labor.

It is important to take care of your physical and mental health. The good news is that when you take care of one area, other areas also benefit. For example, exercise is good for your physical health, but it also has significant mental health benefits. The same with eating healthy and sleeping more. You can also add in things like journaling and meditation, which are also good for your physical and mental health. When you meditate or practice mindfulness, you are essentially removing yourself from the stresses of the day and allowing yourself to just focus on yourself. It gives you mental clarity and you will find that you will feel a lot less stressed out when you have completed your meditation or your mindfulness practices. You don't even need to take out large blocks of time in order to do this. A few minutes a day is enough to see significant benefits.

Another important thing to do for your overall health, as well as your mental health, is to ensure that you have a support structure around you. Having family and friends around you who understand the journey and are willing to be there for you and support you is a valuable resource. It helps you to feel less alone and ensures that people will be there to help you in areas that you might need assistance with. Simply having people there who you can talk to, spend time with, and enjoy yourself with allows you to create balance in your life and live a life full of enjoyment. Nobody is an island, so it is important to ensure that you are building social relationships and a community structure around yourself. This does mean you will need to take time in your day to spend with your loved ones so that they know they are valued. When times get tough, these are the people that are going to be with you, supporting you and loving you. It is more than just creating a network of people who can connect with you professionally, but connecting on a deeper level so that you know that you are understood on that level. Make sure that you are blocking our time in your day to connect with your friends and family. You'll find that on days where you prioritize your mental and physical health, you feel a lot more productive and like you can take on the world, which means that you will be more successful in your real estate journey.

Chapter 9:

Property Management for Beginners

When you invest in real estate, you are essentially purchasing a piece of property. This property needs to be maintained in order to continuously see revenue coming in. Knowing how to manage your properties will allow you to become a more successful real estate investor.

Basics of Managing Rental Properties

When you own a property and are looking to rent it out to tenants in order to make an income, you essentially become a property manager. This means that you'll be responsible for making sure that your tenants are happy and all regulations are being followed, the rent is collected, maintenance issues are resolved, and that you are seeking tenants for any vacant units. You will need to have a budget for your different properties and ensure that you are managing the budget effectively and hitting any revenue goals that you might have set for yourself. When you rent out your property, it is not a form of passive income because you will need to be actively involved to ensure that your tenants are happy and that you are getting paid. You have to focus on marketing the property, upkeep, and ensuring that your tenants are happy. You can do this on your own or you can hire a property manager to take care of all of these tasks. Property managers come at a cost but it is valuable to have this person on your team if you have multiple properties or if you are looking to make your real estate investment more passive.

Once you have the property in your possession, it becomes time for you to start looking for tenants and marketing the property to ensure that you're attracting the right people. The first thing you will need to do is ensure that the property meets all laws and regulations and is actually safe for people to live in. Hiring an inspector is the best way to go because these are professionals and they can give you a clearance certificate so that you have proof that your property is up to code. You will also need to start researching your desired tenant so that you can target your marketing towards this type of person. Many first-time property investors think the best way to go is to simply market to everybody so that they have a wider net. However, when you try and be relatable to every person, you end up being unable to relate to all of them.

Start thinking about what your ideal tenant would look like. You need to be realistic, based on the location and size of your property, and the local amenities. For example, if you have a one-bedroom apartment in the city, this is not going to suit the needs of a couple with three kids. This means your target market would be single professional people who work in the city, students, or perhaps couples just starting their journey together.

Once you know who your ideal tenants are going to be you can start designing your property to suit their needs. On top of that when you put out marketing and advertising you will use descriptions that will draw in that type of person. You can highlight the fact that it is close to the city and business centers for the professional person who might want to rent in that area. You could highlight that it is close to bars and restaurants which means students and younger people would be more inclined to this type of apartment. You would also highlight that it's close to things like transportation and other amenities.

While all of these things might not be something that a couple with children might be looking for, it is definitely something that the aforementioned groups of people would be.

Knowing who your tenants will be also helps you to discover how much rent you should be charging and what kind of amenities and benefits you can add to the property. When you are trying to figure out how much rent to charge, it is a good idea to have a look at similar properties in the area to find out how much they are charging. This way you can price competitively and you know how much your demographic of people are willing to pay. On top of that, you will need to figure out whether you want to have a short-term rental or a long-term rental. Short-term is like vacation rentals where people are in and out every week. If this is something you want to do you need to make sure that your property has the amenities necessary to facilitate this type of activity. For example, you will need to make sure that the decor is stylish and trendy so that it attracts people. You will also need to provide items to meet basic needs such as soaps, conditioners, and shampoos, and have the property cleaned regularly. If you're looking into a long-term rental, you might not need to furnish the apartment as the prospective tenants would have their own furniture. This would mean that it is a more passive form of investing because you only need to get involved should there be a maintenance issue or other issue with the property. All of this information will help you to figure out how you're going to market yourself to the target audience.

Whenever you are marketing something it is important to highlight what is different and unique about it. You want to make sure that your property stands apart from the rest so highlighting exactly what makes it unique ensures that people can differentiate between your rental and someone else's. This unique factor could be the location, style characteristics, amenities, or decor. It is also important that you put your best foot forward when you are advertising and marketing. In order to do this, you will need to stage your property well so that it looks inviting and attractive. Then you will need to take well-lit, quality photographs and show the space accurately, to market yourself on property websites or social media. You will also need to write out an accurate description so people know what they are getting into. Make sure the description highlights the important aspects of the property and uses key descriptive words.

It is also important to remember that word-of-mouth is one of the most crucial aspects of marketing yourself in the property game. If people enjoyed their stay at your rental, it means that they will be willing to talk about it. If you think back to all the recommendations from your friends and family that you actually went through, you'll recognize that we all prefer word-of-mouth recommendations from people that we know and trust. When you make the effort to ensure that your guests or tenants have a wonderful stay in your property, it is more likely that they will tell others about it and you will get return customers as well as new customers based on the word-of-mouth reviews. This means that you do not have to spend as much money on marketing if you already have this base of people who want to stay at your property.

Finding and Dealing With Tenants

Once you know exactly how to market to potential tenants, you will need to know how to deal with them. When you are a first-time real estate investor, you must find the right tenants so that the process is easier and less stressful for you. It is definitely not about finding the first people who are willing to rent out your property because just because people are available and willing to pay does not mean there's going to be a good partnership between you and them. The goal is to have tenants who are going to take care of your property so that you will not need to pay exorbitant amounts of money for maintenance and repairs. You will also want people who are going to respect the property and their neighbors. If you speak to any real estate investor, they probably have quite a few stories of nightmare tenants that made their life so much more difficult than it needed to be.

Marketing yourself right is the first step in finding tenants. This will allow them to come to you so that you have access to their details and can do a background check and an interview with them. It is really important that you conduct an interview so you can get to know them on a personal level and understand their personalities as well as their values.

Once you have found a tenant that you think is the right fit, the process doesn't stop there because you need to make sure that you are doing a screening to ensure that your tenant will be able to pay the rent as well as not having any legal aspects that may prohibit them from living on the property and fulfilling their duties. Doing some screening including background and credit checks is important to make sure that your tenant will be responsible and ensure that they will be able to pay the rent. It is also a good idea to ask them for references from other places they have stayed so that you can get a better idea of what kind of tenants they are. If they do not have people who are willing to vouch for them, this is a bad sign and could lead you to signing a lease with people who are not going to take care of the property and will not respect the rules and regulations that you have laid out for your rental.

It is essential that the tenant onboarding is a smooth process once you have found the people who you want to live in your property. Legal aspects come into play here so you will need to make sure that your lease agreement is solid and legally binding. It is a good idea to get your lawyer involved here to make sure that there aren't any holes in the contract and agreement. The onboarding process should provide your tenant with all the information they would need so it might be a good idea to create an easy-to-read document so they are aware of what is expected of them and what is expected of you.

Later on down the line if there are any complaints or tenant issues it is important that you hold up your end of the bargain and ensure that you are taking care of these in a timely fashion within the bounds of the tenant agreement. While it is important to choose the right tenant, it is also important that you are a good landlord and ensure that you are providing a good experience for the people living on your property. It is easier to find good quality tenants if you have a good reputation as a landlord. If there ever is a complaint, try to ensure that the problem is resolved as quickly as possible. Ensure that you have a healthy relationship with your tenants and this will make the entire rental process much easier and enjoyable for everybody involved.

Maintenance and Financial Management

Being able to maintain your property and manage your finances is key when you are investing in real estate. It is so easy to avoid the maintenance of a property because you want to save money or perhaps things don't look that bad on the outside but this is a huge mistake. A small crack is easy to fix, but also easy to ignore. However, one small bump or extra pressure on that crack can make it grow into a huge one. This is going to take significantly more time, effort, and money to fix than if it was just repaired at the beginning. This thought pattern can be applied to any kind of maintenance on a property. Small things that are brushed under the rug will turn into much bigger things that are more difficult to ignore and will cost you a lot more money to fix.

When you are bringing in an income from your properties, it is important to understand that there are going to be expenses and not all of their revenue equals profit. You will need to put some money aside for the maintenance of the property. Putting a little bit aside every month is the best way to do this so that it's not an overwhelming amount that you are putting away. If it fits in the budget, then you know exactly how much money is profit and how much money you are using for maintenance and other expenses. When something does pop up that needs to be fixed, you will have the money to do it immediately. You don't have to worry about taking out a loan or completely ignoring the issue. Having a maintenance schedule is also really important so that you can take care of monthly and yearly maintenance as it needs to be done. This way there will be fewer issues that pop up and you will be sure that your tenants are happy and well cared for as they stay with you.

Financial management is an important aspect of managing your property, and ensuring that it is running well. As a property manager, you will need to create a budget for each one of your properties so you know how much money you need to put back into them in order to maintain and run things properly. You will also need a strategy for rent collection and ensuring that your tenants pay you on time so you can take care of all the other financial aspects of your property. If you have taken out a mortgage to pay for it, then you'll need to make sure that you make your mortgage payments on time as well as pay for utilities and other bills. It is a good idea to track expenses so that you are fully aware of how much you are spending on the property so your budget is completely accurate and if there is something that looks a little fishy, or you are spending too much money in a certain area, you can amend the budget to ensure that you are only spending what is necessary.

Maintaining your rental property maintenance schedule and finances can be a bit tricky so it is a good idea to look at what technology can be utilized in order to make this a lot easier for you. Technology is such an important tool when you're trying to automate things to ensure that you are spending time on what is necessary. It also streamlines the operations and makes sure communication is enhanced on every level. This means that tasks can be done more efficiently without you having to do things manually all the time. This leads to your renters and tenants being a lot happier with the service they are getting because things are done at a more efficient pace

You can use technology in various areas of your real estate business, and it can be used for a ton of different tasks. For example, you can use spreadsheets to make the tracking processes a lot easier when you are creating a budget or even doing a maintenance schedule. You will have everything on the spreadsheet and you can quickly have a look at what is going on within your properties at a glance. This allows you to have all the data available so you can make better decisions and plan strategically for the future. You can also use technology to automate communication so that your customers and tenants are always aware of what is going on. Automatic emails and messaging systems allow you to send information and even marketing material to your relevant contacts to ensure that communication is streamlined.

If you use a platform like Airbnb, or another short-term rental platform to advertise your property, these will already come integrated with the various tools and technology that you can use to your advantage. You will be able to gain access to things like analytics and automated messaging tools so you can make things a lot easier for yourself. This can also be integrated into an external calendar so that you are aware of how many people are staying in your various properties and the dates they will be staying. This lowers the risk of double booking and also ensures that you are always aware of what is going on with your properties.

New technologies are always coming out, so it is important to do your research and find out exactly which forms of technology you would like to integrate into your real estate strategy. Have a look at reviews and also get insights from your mentors and network to see what types of apps or technology they are using so you can get a better idea of what is popular and why it is popular. Many of the platforms and apps will allow free trials, which means that you can see if something is for you before you make the purchase. It is always a good idea to do this, so you can get a good feel of how it is going to integrate into your overall plan before you commit. Once you have found the right technology for you, you'll find that things are a lot easier and more automated.

We've covered many different topics within this book, and in the next chapter, we are going to be diving into how we can bring everything together so you can build a personalized real estate portfolio and ensure that your investment plan is comprehensive and future-proof.

Chapter 10:

Bringing It All Together

The goal of investing in real estate is to bring it into the other areas of your life so that you can reach your overall financial goals. This shouldn't be a completely separate aspect from the rest of your life because you need to integrate it so that you can create a balanced life as well as ensure that whatever you are doing in your investment journey will serve you in your personal life as well. Remember that every aspect of your life is connected so making sure that your investment goals match up to your personal goals is essential. This will lead to a more sustainable investment journey.

Developing a Comprehensive Investment Plan

It is really important to make sure that your investment plan aligns with your personal financial health. These two aspects are not going to be separate as you want the money that you make through your investments to feed into your personal finances so that you can live the life that you want. This means that you are going to need to create a personal financial budget and ensure that your investment fits into it. Understanding what you want on a personal level will help you to decide how you should be investing through real estate and what types of investments are best going to suit your overall goals.

You will first need to have a look at your current financial situation to decide how much you can actually invest and what is going to work best for you. If you don't have a lot of money to spare for your investment it might be a good idea to start thinking about how to increase your revenue or your income so that you can save more money and then put that into your investments. You might need to start by investing in things that require less start-up capital and then move on to bigger investments as you grow your wealth.

It can be tempting to throw all of your money into your investments when you first start on your investment journey but this is not a good idea. You will need to make sure that your personal financial health is taken care of so that there is no additional pressure put on your investment. For example, if you are currently in a lot of debt then it is more important that you work to pay off the debt rather than funneling all your money into your investment. Your debt is always going to be something that is going to hold you back until you make a plan to work it off. This doesn't mean that you can't invest if you do have debt but you need to make it a priority to pay off the debt so that it doesn't have the chance to come back and bite you in the end.

It is also a good idea to create an emergency fund for your personal finances to ensure that if there ever is an emergency you have the money to pay for it. This emergency fund should be three to six months' worth of your expenses. If something unexpected were to happen then you have the money to pay for it and you don't need to sell off your investment or take out large loans in order to cater to the emergency. This simply helps you to be more prepared for unexpected situations in life and ensures that your finances can continue to grow in a healthy manner.

Something else that you need to consider is your retirement and how close you are to retirement age. The older you get, the lower your risk tolerance is, which means that you can't make as many risky decisions with your finances. It is true that with more risk comes more reward when it comes to investing but when you don't have that much time it becomes more dangerous to invest in risky options. When you have a long time until retirement age it is a lot easier to make risky investments that could potentially bring in more money because you have so much more time until you have to retire. Think about your risk tolerance and how much money you have as well as how much time you have for your investment before you start making them.

Once you understand where you are financially then you can start setting goals for your investments. Think about why you are investing and what you would like to do with the money that you make through your real estate investments. You might be using real estate investing as a way to have a secure retirement or perhaps you wanted an additional source of income so that you can travel more or secure your children's futures. Understanding what the ultimate goals are for your investment means that you can create goals and milestones throughout the process so that you can measure your progress and ensure that your current investment plan is continuously serving you.

Building a Personalized Real Estate Portfolio

Every person has a different investment style based on their goals, risk tolerance, and preferences. One of the biggest mistakes that new investors make is that they find an investor they like and start to copy their investment style.This might sound like a good idea because you are copying the style of another successful investor but it never works because you do not have the experience, knowledge, personality, or investment style of somebody else. The person you are aiming to copy is making investments based on what they want out of them and there's no guarantee that you have the exact same goals or lifestyle as that person. That person might also have more financial resources and opportunities than you have access to at this time. What could be working out brilliantly for them could be detrimental to your investments and overall finances.

Your investment strategy needs to be unique to you, based on doing your own research and understanding yourself and your finances. You will need to create your own investment portfolio based on your own needs and resources. It is important to have a diversified investment portfolio to make sure that your investments are secure and that your finances are not going to be at risk of something negative happening in a specific market or type of real estate. There are many different types of investment styles out there as well as many different types of real estate investment income sources. You may be somebody who is looking to make an income through your investment and this means that purchasing properties to rent out would be a good investment strategy for you. Perhaps you would prefer a more growth-oriented investment where you purchase properties at a lower price and allow them to appreciate in value before you sell them for a profit. You could also be somebody who prefers a more balanced approach and wants to incorporate both of these aspects into your investment style.

Remember that it is going to be important that you choose property types that align with your personal preferences and overall investment objectives. If you do not want to be a landlord then it's not going to make sense for you to purchase an apartment block where you have to find tenants and continuously perform landlord tasks. You also might not have the risk tolerance needed to invest in something like commercial real estate even though this type of investment does bring in a lot of money. You have full agency over your investment and the type you want to purchase or invest in but it is important that you have a look at yourself and understand your own needs before you jump into any kind of investment.

When you are a property investor, it is not simply about buying a property at the beginning and then leaving it at that. As you grow as an investor you change and gain more knowledge and this means your business or investment style might start to differ from what you first started out with. It is important that you do regular portfolio reviews to make sure that your investments are performing as they should and to ensure that your current investments are meeting your current lifestyle goals and objectives. The real estate market is something that is always changing and if you simply stick to the same strategy from day one you are probably not going to make as much money as you would like to and you could be putting yourself at unnecessary risk.

It is important to understand that the market is continuously changing and you need to make decisions in response to this. Reevaluating your investment plan every few months helps you to stay on top of what is happening in the market and in your own personal financial plan. You might decide that the investment you thought was a good idea is not performing as it should have and you need to sell it or restructure your investment plan. This is a normal part of investing and it is important to factor it into your schedule to make sure that your investments are always going to be performing at their best. It is easy to get complacent especially if your investment portfolio has been performing well without any restructuring. However, it is important to not get lazy when it comes to reviewing your investment plan and understanding how it fits into your current financial goals. As you move through life, your financial goals will change so this means the way you invest also needs to shift. If you make this a habit, it's going to be a lot easier for you to continuously review your investments and you will likely get much better results by doing this.

Continued Learning and Adaptation

The truth is that investing is something that you will continue to learn about. Even investment professionals who have been in the investment game for many years are still learning and growing. There will never be a point where you are so good at investing that there will be nothing to learn. With time you will definitely get better with your decision-making and your investments but this doesn't mean that the learning and growth stops there.

Remember that the real estate investment market is always changing and there are new trends coming in and out. On top of that, economic factors are continuously impacting the real estate market and you can never predict what is going to happen in the economy 50 years from now. What worked for you 10 years ago might be detrimental to your investment portfolio right now. This is why continuous learning and ensuring that you are up-to-date with any legal or regulatory changes will help you stay on top of your investments.

It might seem overwhelming to be continuously learning and growing but this is an important part of being a human. Rather than looking at it as something that is inconvenient, you can look at it as an opportunity to become better and more well-equipped. As humans, we are always supposed to be learning and growing throughout our lives and it is never supposed to be something that is capped by age or experience. You can take the same mentality and apply it to your investments to ensure that you are getting the best out of it and always looking for new areas in which you can learn and grow.

These days it is so easy to access learning materials cheaply or for free. Even if you do have to make some sort of monetary investment into learning more about the real estate market, then it is worth it. Remember to always be reading books, signing up for courses, webinars, and seminars, and getting knowledge through mentorships and talking to other people who are in the real estate investment space. If you make it a habit to learn and grow in your real estate investment space then this will be something that you do almost subconsciously. You will always be looking for new information and you'll be reading articles, books, websites, and watching videos all the time which is going to feed into gaining more knowledge in this area. Eventually, it will become second nature and this means that you can learn and grow without even having to think about it. You will quickly see that it becomes so much more enjoyable to do this when you get to witness the benefits of it on your own real estate investment journey.

Gaining more information and continuously being flexible with your investment will allow you to become more adaptable to the evolving markets. I have seen many investors who get quite put off by the changes in the market but the truth is this comes with opportunities. Rather than looking at a change as something that needs to be avoided, you can look at it as something to lean into so you can be an investor who finds opportunities to grow and increase their investments. The changing markets can be something positive because something new always means that there is a new opportunity. It might take a while for this new aspect of investment to gain traction but if you have already learned about it and started implementing and leaning into the changes this means that you will be at the forefront of the growth and will be the one that benefits the most from it.

If you look at big companies like Microsoft when they first started, people had their doubts about this technology that was disrupting the market. It took quite a long time before it was adopted as commonplace and only a few people would've invested into it at the beginning. They saw that change was coming and they made sure that they put themselves in a position to support the change and invest in something that had potential future growth. The people who invested right at the beginning are the people who saw the most growth in their investment portfolios because they only needed to invest a small amount to allow this to grow in the future. They took the risk in the changing market and saw huge payoffs from it. While this is a completely different thing than investing in real estate, the same principle applies. When things start changing and shifting in the market it is important to make educated decisions and not be scared of what these changes might imply. You could be on the precipice of investments that make you a lot of money and ensure that you can reach your personal financial goals. If there is something new that pops up it is important to do your research before you decide what you are going to do about it but never back away just because something is changing or feels new.

Investing in real estate is definitely a journey and it is an exciting one. It gives you the opportunity to grow your wealth and ensure that you are providing for yourself, reaching your goals, and taking care of your family. It puts you in a position where you get to be in control of your finances and you don't have to rely on other people or a regular 9-to-5 job to financially fund your lifestyle. Instead, you are in the driver's seat and you get to be the one who is in charge of everything that happens in your life and in your financial future. This is a very exciting journey that you are about to embark on and it is something that you will look back on and be so thankful that you got started when you did.

Conclusion

Now that you have reached the end of the book, this does not mean that your real estate investment journey has come to an end. In fact, it is just the beginning and that is the exciting part. Now is the time when you get to take everything that you've learned and put it into practice so that you can reach maximum success. There have been a lot of tips and tricks as well as guidelines throughout this book that can help you in your real estate investment journey. This journey is not something that happens quickly so you will continuously be on the path of learning and growing as you become a better investor. Different tips and tricks will work for different areas and different spaces within your real estate investment journey. You can use this book as a guidebook where you go back to the relevant topics as you need it. This way you always have access to the important information to help you take your next steps.

I would suggest that you think about what your next step is on your investment journey and go back to the relevant chapter so that you can refresh your memory on the topic. This way you can start thinking about how you can use the information to become a successful real estate investor. At this point, you've gotten a good overview of all the information you need, so you know what to expect from this journey. Going back and diving a little deeper when it comes time to actually implement that information is an essential part of the process.

Remember that real estate investment is an ever-changing field which means that you will always need to be learning and growing. This book is designed to give you the foundational understanding of exactly what you need to do to get started, but there's always going to be more to learn. Getting a mentor and signing up for classes, books, and podcasts can help you to deepen your knowledge and get more relevant information as time goes on. This will allow you to create a strategy that is going to be the most beneficial to your real estate investment journey. The goal is to always stay informed and flexible so that you can change up your strategy and approach based on what is going on in the market and whatever new information is available. Being a flexible investor is the pathway to allow you to become a successful investor.

I want to take this time to thank you for diving into this topic and reading the book. I have witnessed so many beginner investors learn the right approach and become successful through implementing the guidelines and advice that have been laid out in this book. I hope that you will become a success in your own life with the power of real estate investing. This is a lifelong journey that can open so many opportunities for you, so I hope that you really grab the bull by the horns and make it a priority to attain financial freedom through real estate investing.

If you found this book valuable, I would really appreciate it if you wrote a review. This way more people who are getting started on their real estate investment journey will be able to find it. This expands my reach and allows more people to jump on board and become successful. I wish you luck on your investment journey and know that if you put in the work and implement what you've learned, you will be able to reach your goals and become a successful real estate investor.

References

A guide to real estate risk management. (2023, March 13). Embroker. https://www.embroker.com/blog/real-estate-risk-management/

Adapting to a new commercial real estate landscape. (2024, January 4). Excelsior Capital. https://www.excelsiorgp.com/resources/adapting-to-a-new-commercial-real-estate-landscape/

Araj, V. (2023, December 20). *Capital gains tax on real estate & home sales.* Rocket Mortgage. https://www.rocketmortgage.com/learn/capital-gains-home-sale

Araj, V. (2024, February 15). *Comparative market analysis: A guide.* Rocket Mortgage. https://www.rocketmortgage.com/learn/comparative-market-analysis

Bagla, M. (2023, August 31). *Difference between long term and short term strategies.* Paytm Blog. https://paytm.com/blog/investment/difference-between-long-term-and-short-term-strategies/

Beltran, C. (2023, October 20). *Emerging markets: Identifying and capitalizing on new real estate opportunities.* Linkedin. https://www.linkedin.com/pulse/emerging-markets-identifying-capitalizing-new-real-estate-beltran-gbxvc

Benson, A. (2023, September 12). *Types of real estate investments.* NerdWallet. https://www.nerdwallet.com/article/investing/types-of-real-estate-investments

Bickmore, R. (2019, July 11). *The underlying factors that influence real estate market growth.* Linkedin. https://www.linkedin.com/pulse/underlying-factors-influence-real-estate-market-growth-bickmore/

Bloch, B. J. (2022, August 31). *Diversifying with real estate and infrastructure.* Investopedia. https://www.investopedia.com/articles/stocks/11/real-estate-infrastructure-asset-allocation.asp

Borrowers' rights. (2023). FindLaw. https://www.findlaw.com/realestate/mortgages-equity-loans/borrowers-rights.html

Buttsworth, T. (2023, October 1). *The bedrock of real estate investment: The power of a solid budget.* Linkedin. https://www.linkedin.com/pulse/bedrock-real-estate-investment-power-solid-budget-talisha-buttsworth/

Catmull, J. (2022, December 3). *How to invest in real estate on a budget.* Forbes. https://www.forbes.com/sites/jaimecatmull/2022/12/03/the-machine-that-builds-a-future/?sh=703baacd3c19

Chari, V. (2022, May 10). *7 ways to minimize risk in a real estate investment.* Forbes Advisor INDIA. https://www.forbes.com/advisor/in/investing/7-ways-to-minimize-risk-in-a-real-estate-investment/

Chen, J. (2023, April 24). *Real estate: Definition, types, how to invest in it.* Investopedia. https://www.investopedia.com/terms/r/realestate.asp

Choosing short-term or long-term real estate investments. (2020, October 28). Asset Based Lending. https://www.abl1.net/blog/short-or-long-term-real-estate-investing/

Clemon, D. (2022, March). *A list of rules for home buyers working with real estate agents.* The Balance. https://www.thebalancemoney.com/rules-for-working-with-agents-1798904

Clifford, R. (2017, July 19). *6 economic principles that affect real estate valuations.* RDC Appraisals, LLC. https://www.rdcappraisals.com/6-economic-principles-affect-real-estate-valuations/

Complete guide to efficient real estate market analysis. (n.d.). Placer.ai. https://www.placer.ai/guides/real-estate-market-analysis

Coulter, J. (2022). *Real-time market monitoring finds signs of brewing U.S. housing bubble.* Dallasfed. https://www.dallasfed.org/research/economics/2022/0329

Crace, M. (2024, January 19). *What is a mortgage? The basics for beginners.* Rocket Mortgage. https://www.rocketmortgage.com/learn/what-is-a-mortgage

Deming, M. (2018, September 20). *7 effective ways to market your rental property.* Avail.

https://www.avail.co/education/articles/marketing-tips-for-your-rental-listings

Distinct differences between national and local housing markets. (2017, August 28). Winnipeg Regional Real Estate News. https://www.winnipegregionalrealestatenews.com/publications/real-estate-news/3041

Do your investments match your financial goals? (2023, April 3). US Bank. https://www.usbank.com/financialiq/invest-your-money/investment-strategies/do-your-investments-match-your-personal-financial-goals.html

8 proven professional networking tips for realtors. (2021, December 2). KADO Networks. https://www.kadonetworks.com/blog/use-these-ideas-to-bring-your-real-estate-networking

Eisner, C. (2022, November 17). *What is property maintenance?* MaintainX. https://www.getmaintainx.com/learning-center/property-maintenance/

Emerging trends in real estate 2022. (2022). https://www.pwc.com/us/en/industries/financial-services/asset-wealth-management/real-estate/emerging-trends-in-real-estate.html

Emerging trends in real estate: A comprehensive guide to the future of property investment. (2023, August 23). Global Property Shows. https://globalpropertyshows.com/emerging-trends-in-real-estate/

Esajian, J. (2021, November 8). *The best tax benefits of real estate investing.* FortuneBuilders.

https://www.fortunebuilders.com/real-estate-investing-tax-benefits/

Esajian, P. (2016, December 27). *The unwritten rules of real estate networking.* FortuneBuilders. https://www.fortunebuilders.com/rules-of-real-estate-networking/

Esajian, P. (2021a, January 22). *Understanding the four phases of the real estate cycle.* FortuneBuilders. https://www.fortunebuilders.com/real-estate-cycle/

Esajian, P. (2021b, February 12). *5 real estate goals for the SMART investor.* FortuneBuilders. https://www.fortunebuilders.com/5-real-estate-business-goals/

Esajian, P. (2022, November 2). *How to build business credit for real estate.* FortuneBuilders. https://www.fortunebuilders.com/build-real-estate-business-credit/

Eversole, D. (2023, August 22). *Understanding real estate market cycles: Timing your investments.* Linkedin. https://www.linkedin.com/pulse/understanding-real-estate-market-cycles-timing-your-dillon-eversole/

External factors that impact on property sales. (2015, November 3). Durbanville-Property. https://durbanville-property.co.za/external-factors-that-impact-on-property-sales/

Factors affecting property value. (2023, August 11). Domus.net. https://www.domus.net/article?articleID=35

Factors affecting residential property valuation. (2021, August 24). Homecapital. https://homecapital.in/blog/factors-that-affect-property-valuation

Ferraro, J. (2023, May). *The importance of networking in real estate: Key strategies for success.* Linkedin. https://www.linkedin.com/pulse/importance-networking-real-estate-key-strategies-success-jo-ferraro/

Financial planning for real estate investments. (2024, January 7). Meru Accounting. https://www.meruaccounting.com/blog/financial-planning-for-real-estate/

Find the best properties on the market. (2023). TruVest. https://www.truvest.io/article/2024-mitigating-risks-in-real-estate

5 powerful reasons to invest in yourself. (n.d.). The British School of Excellence. https://thebritishschoolofexcellence.com/life-skills/5-powerful-reasons-to-invest-in-yourself/

Folger, J. (2023, July 24). *Comparative market analysis.* Investopedia. https://www.investopedia.com/terms/c/comparative-market-analysis.asp

Fonville, M. (2023, April 1). *9 crucial components of an investment portfolio review.* Covenant Wealth. https://www.covenantwealthadvisors.com/post/9-crucial-components-investment-portfolio-review

Freeze, P. (2022, August 2). *Classification of real estate: The 3 types of investment markets explained.* Bay Property Management Group. https://www.baymgmtgroup.com/blog/classification-of-real-estate-the-3-types-of-investment/

Freudenberg, D. (2020, April 6). *The psychology behind real estate investing risks: Do you have what it takes?* Think Save Retire. https://thinksaveretire.com/real-estate-investing-risks/

Future home value calculator - free online home value calculator. (2018, December 27). What Is the Value of My Home? https://www.whatisvalueofmyhome.com/future-home-value-calculator/

Future value calculator, definition, and examples. (2022, February 1). Bungalow. https://bungalow.com/articles/what-is-future-value

Government and real estate. (2019, February 12). The CE Shop. https://www.theceshop.com/agent-essentials/blog/government-and-real-estate

Guide to staying up-to-date on real estate market trends. (2023, August 22). RealtyTimes. https://realtytimes.com/consumeradvice/ask-the-expert/item/1047521-guide-to-staying-up-to-date-on-real-estate-market-trends

Gupta, R. (2023, October 29). Understanding property market cycles for smart investment choices. *The Economic Times.* https://economictimes.indiatimes.com/markets/stocks/news/understanding-property-market-cycles-for-smart-investment-choices/articleshow/104795000.cms

Henson, T. (2022, September 27). *Types of real estate investment risks investors should know.* Beach Front Property Management. https://bfpminc.com/6-types-of-real-estate-investment-risks-that-investors-need-to-know/

How changing demographics impact the real estate market. (2023, October 6). Excelsior Capital. https://www.excelsiorgp.com/resources/how-changing-demographics-impact-the-real-estate-market/

How do you grow from success and failure in real estate niches? (n.d.). Linkedin. https://www.linkedin.com/advice/3/how-do-you-grow-from-success-failure-real-estate-niches

How does real estate fit into your financial plan? (2022, November 12). Fee-Based Wealth Management and Financial Planning. https://centurawealth.com/blog/how-does-real-estate-fit-into-your-financial-plan

How does the location of a house impact its value? (2023, March 30). Financialexpress. https://www.financialexpress.com/money/how-does-the-location-of-a-house-impacts-its-value-3026927/

How to build a support system for success in the real estate industry. (2023, May 23). Kurby. https://blog.kurby.ai/how-to-build-a-support-system-for-success-in-the-real-estate-industry/

How to build and maintain a strong credit for a favourable home loan. (2023, October 17). Financialexpress. https://www.financialexpress.com/money/how-to-build-and-maintain-a-strong-credit-for-a-favourable-home-loan-3274855/

How to effectively manage cash flow for your real estate business. (2023, June 26). Linkedin. https://www.linkedin.com/pulse/how-effectively-manage-cash-flow-your-real-estate-taiwo/

How to leverage life insurance to invest in real estate. (2022, June 23). Safepacific.com. https://safepacific.com/how-to-leverage-life-insurance-to-invest-in-real-estate/

How to mitigate risks in real estate investments. (n.d.). Linkedin. https://www.linkedin.com/pulse/how-mitigate-risks-real-estate-investments-calcap-lending/

Importance of location in real estate: Key factors to consider when investing. (n.d.). AssureShift. https://www.assureshift.in/blog/importance-of-location-in-real-estate

Importance of regulatory framework and policies in real estate. (2023, January 18). Timesproperty.com. https://timesproperty.com/news/post/government-institutional-policies-in-real-estate-growth-blid3716

Kagan, J. (2021, February 25). *Mortgage*. Investopedia. https://www.investopedia.com/terms/m/mortgage.asp

Keilar, H. (2023, December 23). *Loan modification vs. refinance*. Rocket Mortgage. https://www.rocketmortgage.com/learn/loan-modification-vs-refinance

Koren, L. (2021, January 25). *7 ways to maintain good credit for your next rental property investment*. Luxury Property Care.

https://luxurypropertycare.com/good-credit-for-next-rental-property-investment/

Landon, D. (n.d.). *The top 10 metrics every real estate investor should know (and why).* Stessa. https://www.stessa.com/blog/10-real-estate-investing-metrics/

Lands and Homes India. (2023, May 29). *Factors that affect the value of a property.* Linkedin. https://www.linkedin.com/pulse/factors-affect-value-property-landsandhomes/

Langager, C. (2023, March 12). *Is it true that you can sell your home and not pay capital gains tax?* Investopedia. https://www.investopedia.com/ask/answers/06/capitalgainhomesale.asp

Leveraging technology for real estate brokers: A game-changer in the industry | GAAR blog. (2023, September 5). Greater Albuquerque Association of REALTORS®. https://www.gaar.com/blog/article/leveraging-technology-for-real-estate-brokers-a-game-changer-in-the-industr

Levinson, C. (2020, October 15). *8 key components you can expect to see in your mortgage agreement.* HomeLight Blog. https://www.homelight.com/blog/buyer-mortgage-agreement/

Loan modification laws. (2012, October 24). LegalMatch Law Library. https://www.legalmatch.com/law-library/article/loan-modification-lawyers.html

Luna, A. (2023, September 27). *Leveraging technology for enhanced property management: Insights from Coastline Equity.* Coastline Equity. https://www.coastlineequity.net/leveraging-technology-for-enhanced-property-management-insights-from-coastline-equity

Manjrekar, N. (2023, August 2). *10 types of properties in real estate and what they mean for you.* PropertyCloud. https://propertycloud.in/blog/types-of-properties-in-real-estate/

Manzolillo, N. (2022a, August 18). *The 4 stages of the real estate cycle & how to navigate them.* ButterflyMX. https://butterflymx.com/blog/real-estate-cycle/

Manzolillo, N. (2022b, October 12). *8 real estate risks & what you should watch out for.* ButterflyMX. https://butterflymx.com/blog/real-estate-risk/

Market indicator. (n.d.). Corporate Finance Institute. https://corporatefinanceinstitute.com/resources/career-map/sell-side/capital-markets/market-indicator/

Market rent: The impact of market rent on AFFO: Key considerations. (2024, March 9). FasterCapital. https://fastercapital.com/content/Market-rent--The-Impact-of-Market-Rent-on-AFFO--Key-Considerations.html

Martin, E. J. (2023, January). *Common contingencies in real estate explained.* Bankrate. https://www.bankrate.com/real-estate/contingency-clause/

Martin, S. (2023, July 17). *Your "local" housing market: More national than you might expect.* Due Diligence. https://warrington.ufl.edu/due-diligence/2023/07/17/your-local-housing-market-more-national-than-you-might-expect/

Marvin, M. (2023). *Building resilience in the real estate industry: Navigating economic volatility.* Linkedin. https://www.linkedin.com/pulse/building-resilience-real-estate-industry-navigating-economic-marvin/

Matoza, J. (2022, October 17). *4 main factors affecting the real estate market.* Linkedin. https://www.linkedin.com/pulse/4-main-factors-affecting-real-estate-market-jacqueline-matoza/

Mburugu, C. (2020, June 23). *Short term vs long term investments in real estate: Which is better for you?* Mashvisor Real Estate Blog. https://www.mashvisor.com/blog/short-term-vs-long-term-investments-real-estate/

Merrill, T. (2015, October 5). *Alternative real estate financing: The key to a successful business.* FortuneBuilders. https://www.fortunebuilders.com/alternative-financing-the-key-to-a-successful-real-estate-business/

Merrill, T. (2022, June 17). *Top 10 platforms for your real estate social network.* FortuneBuilders. https://www.fortunebuilders.com/real-estate-social-network/

Meyer, S. (2023, September 17). *Everything you need to know about due diligence in real estate.* The Zebra.

https://www.thezebra.com/resources/home/due-diligence-real-estate/

Mittal, V., & Schaposnik, L. P. (2023). Housing market forecasts via stock market indicators. *Heliyon, 9*(5), e16286. https://doi.org/10.1016/j.heliyon.2023.e16286

Mortgage answers. (n.d.). Consumer Financial Protection Bureau. https://www.consumerfinance.gov/consumer-tools/mortgages/answers/key-terms/

Murdock, C. (2021, April 4). *Steps to onboarding a new tenant.* Rent Spree. https://www.rentspree.com/blog/onboarding-new-tenant

Navigating the home loan process: A step-by-step guide. (2023, May 22). Keller Home Loans. https://kwlends.com/navigating-the-home-loan-process-a-step-by-step-guide/

Nguyen, J. (2023, June 12). *4 key factors that drive the real estate market.* Investopedia. https://www.investopedia.com/articles/mortages-real-estate/11/factors-affecting-real-estate-market.asp

9 effective ways to find the best real estate investing mentor. (2023, August 3). SyndicationPro. https://syndicationpro.com/blog/effective-ways-find-best-real-estate-investing-mentor

Ouwens Cassidy Real Estate. (2022, November 28). *Creating a budget for your investment property.* Linkedin. https://www.linkedin.com/pulse/creating-budget-your-investment-property-/

Palomar, E. (2023, May 4). *What is comparative market analysis (CMA) in real estate?* Indeed. https://www.indeed.com/career-advice/career-development/what-is-a-cma-in-real-estate

Parodi, M. W. (2022, March 15). *Real estate taxes: A complete guide to the basics.* The Motley Fool. https://www.fool.com/the-ascent/taxes/real-estate-taxes-your-complete-guide/

Peacock, C. (2023, February 20). *How to scale a real-estate business.* Linkedin. https://www.linkedin.com/pulse/how-scale-real-estate-business-cheline-peacock/

Peak Frameworks Team. (2023, May 22). *The 4 types of real estate investments (land, residential, commercial, industrial).* Peak Frameworks. https://www.peakframeworks.com/post/real-estate-types

Pinkasovitch, A. (2021, February 13). *How to value real estate investment property.* Investopedia. https://www.investopedia.com/articles/mortgages-real-estate/11/valuing-real-estate.asp

Pomroy, K. (2022, November 4). *What is the due diligence period in real estate?* Experian. https://www.experian.com/blogs/ask-experian/what-is-due-diligence-period-real-estate/

Prater, M. (2018, October 25). *The ultimate dictionary of real estate terms you should know.* Blog.hubspot.com. https://blog.hubspot.com/sales/real-estate-terms

Prehn, L. (2022, October 18). *10 useful real estate tax credits for developers and investors.* Moskowitz LLP. https://moskowitzllp.com/real-estate-tax-credits-for-developers-investors/

Property law in the United States. (2020, December 26). Wikipedia. https://en.wikipedia.org/wiki/Property_law_in_the_United_States

Property tax basics. (2024). FindLaw. https://www.findlaw.com/realestate/owning-a-home/property-tax-basics.html

Purchase and sale pitfalls: Due diligence and disclosures. (2019, March 8). Schorr Law. https://schorr-law.com/purchase-and-sale-pitfalls-due-diligence-and-disclosures/

Real estate finance law. (2014, February 10). LegalMatch Law Library. https://www.legalmatch.com/law-library/article/real-estate-finance-law.html

Real estate investing strategies. (n.d.). Ameriprise Financial. https://www.ameriprise.com/financial-goals-priorities/investing/real-estate-investing-strategies

Real estate investment strategies for a volatile market. (n.d.). Godrej Properties. https://www.godrejproperties.com/blog/real-estate-investment-strategies-for-a-volatile-market

Real estate investment: Understanding the different property types and investment strategies. (2023, July 31). Linkedin. https://www.linkedin.com/pulse/real-estate-investment-understanding-different-property/

Real estate investments. (n.d.). CFA Institute. https://www.cfainstitute.org/en/membership/professional-development/refresher-readings/real-estate-investments

Real estate law. (n.d.). Goodwin, Gillis & Heck. http://www.gghlawfirm.com/real-estate-law.html

Real estate market analysis: 10 ways to identify emerging neighborhoods. (2023, September 26). REtechnology. https://retechnology.com/article-lists/30825-real-estate-market-analysis-10-ways-to-identify-emerging-neighborhoods

Real estate market size and trends, forecast, 2030. (2023, August 23). Linkedin. https://www.linkedin.com/pulse/real-estate-market-size-trends-forecast-2030/

Real estate networking best practices. (2022, November 4). Market Leader. https://www.marketleader.com/blog/real-estate-networking/

Real estate terms for homebuyers – everything you should know! (2023, May 31). Sobha. https://www.sobha.com/blog/real-estate-terms/

Rees, J. (2023, October 12). *The importance of stress management for real estate agents: How to find balance in a demanding industry.* Linkedin. https://www.linkedin.com/pulse/importance-stress-management-real-estate-agents-how-find-josie-rees-f6tcc/

Richardson, S. (2024, March 19). *What does a property manager do?* Rocket Mortgage.

https://www.rocketmortgage.com/learn/what-does-a-property-manager-do

Riding the wave of market trends: Expert strategies for adapting to a changing real estate landscape – liberty title. (2023, April 21). Libtitle. https://libtitle.com/riding-the-wave-of-market-trends-expert-strategies-for-adapting-to-a-changing-real-estate-landscape/

Robinson, M. (2023, December 12). *Real estate market dynamics: Understanding the recent trends and future predictions.* Linkedin. https://www.linkedin.com/pulse/real-estate-market-dynamics-understanding-recent-trends-robinson-1fmac/

Rohde, J. (n.d.). *How to screen tenants: 6 essential steps.* Stessa. https://www.stessa.com/blog/how-to-screen-tenants/

Rojo, L. (2023, July 11). *Leveraging real estate investment groups for networking.* Green Residential. https://www.greenresidential.com/leveraging-real-estate-investment-groups-for-networking-and-learning/

Santos, S. (2023, March 7). *The importance of cash flow management in real estate.* STRATAFOLIO. https://stratafolio.com/the-importance-of-cash-flow-management-in-real-estate/

Scherer, D. (2017, December 12). *8 types of risk every real estate investor should know about.* Origin Investments. https://origininvestments.com/8-types-risk-every-real-estate-investor-know/

Seabury, C. (2020). *How property taxes are calculated.* Investopedia. https://www.investopedia.com/articles/tax/09/calculate-property-tax.asp

Sell your home the minute you're ready. (n.d.). Opendoor. https://www.opendoor.com/articles/real-estate-terms-you-should-know

Seth, S. (2019). *13 steps of a real estate closing.* Investopedia. https://www.investopedia.com/articles/mortgages-real-estate/10/closing-home-process.asp

Seth, S. (2022, March 19). *The most important factors for investing in real estate.* Investopedia. https://www.investopedia.com/articles/investing/110614/most-important-factors-investing-real-estate.asp

Setting up your build-to-rent properties for success. (n.d.). Property Management Consulting. https://www.propertymanagementconsulting.com/build-to-rent-property-management-consulting-services

Sinha, S. (2023, November 16). *Strategic considerations for successful real estate investments.* Financialexpress. https://www.financialexpress.com/money/strategic-considerations-for-successful-real-estate-investments-3307816/

Smith, J. (2023, September 21). *Timing the real estate market: The best times to invest.* Linkedin. https://www.linkedin.com/pulse/timing-real-estate-market-best-times-invest-javier-smith/

Sopielnikow, K. (2016, May 10). *How to build a real estate network like a pro.* FortuneBuilders.

https://www.fortunebuilders.com/build-a-real-estate-network/

Stojanovska, J. (2023, August 9). *The power of personal development plans for real estate agents.* Linkedin. https://www.linkedin.com/pulse/power-personal-development-plans-real-estate-agents-stojanovska/

Struyk, T. (2021, February 26). *The 5 factors of a "good" location.* Investopedia. https://www.investopedia.com/financial-edge/0410/the-5-factors-of-a-good-location.aspx

Takhar, J. (2023, June 4). *Exploring economic factors for a solid real estate market.* Linkedin. https://www.linkedin.com/pulse/exploring-economic-factors-solid-real-estate-market-jas-takhar/

Taylor, J. (2023, November 29). *Capital gains tax on real estate and home sales.* Kiplinger. https://www.kiplinger.com/taxes/capital-gains-tax-on-real-estate

Thakur, A. (2024, February 27). *Government policies effects on real estate & new initiatives and their impacts.* Linkedin. https://www.linkedin.com/pulse/government-policies-effects-real-estate-new-impacts-aniket-thakur/

Thangavelu, P. (2023, August 16). *Top U.S. housing market indicators.* Investopedia. https://www.investopedia.com/articles/personal-finance/033015/top-us-housing-market-indicators.asp

The impact of demographics on real estate market trends. (2023, June 21). Vraj Tiara. https://vrajtiara.com/the-impact-of-demographics-on-real-estate-market-trends/

The importance of work-life integration for real estate professionals. (2023, May). Kurby. https://blog.kurby.ai/the-importance-of-work-life-integration-for-real-estate-professionals/

TheDataSolution. (2023, January 27). *Real estate data collection: A comprehensive guide to gather and analyze data.* Medium. https://medium.com/@ai.thedatasolution/real-estate-data-collection-a-comprehensive-guide-to-gather-and-analyze-data-5445ea3656be

31 tax deductions real estate investors need to know about. (2022, February 25). Mynd Management. https://www.mynd.co/knowledge-center/10-tax-deductions-often-overlooked-by

Tips & tricks for real estate time management. (2021). Tom Ferry. https://www.tomferry.com/articles/time-management-for-realtors/

Top 6 data collection tips to build a powerful real estate marketplace. (2023, January 17). Habiledata. https://www.habiledata.com/blog/data-collection-tips-for-real-estate-marketplaces/

Top 11 important economic factors affecting housing market. (2019, October 22). PVS. https://pvsbuilders.com/economic-factors-affecting-housing-market/

2 financing alternatives for real estate developers. (2022, February 24). Alter Finance. https://www.alterfinancegroup.com/en/blog/promoters/2-financing-alternatives-for-real-estate-developers/

Understanding home loan basics before you buy. (n.d.). Fannie Mae. https://yourhome.fanniemae.com/buy/understanding-home-loan-basics

Understanding service charge in real estate and facility management. (2023, July 7). Linkedin. https://www.linkedin.com/pulse/understanding-service-charge-real-estate-facility/

Unveiling the hidden costs of real estate: A guide to effective planning. (2023, June 13). Linkedin. https://www.linkedin.com/pulse/unveiling-hidden-costs-real-estate-guide-effective-planning-phoree/

Vasquez, A. (2022, February 17). *Council post: Handling tenant issues and complaints in rentals.* Forbes. https://www.forbes.com/sites/forbesbusinesscouncil/2023/02/17/handling-tenant-issues-and-complaints-in-rentals/?sh=4121c13dafb7

Virginia property and real estate laws. (2016). Find Law. https://www.findlaw.com/state/virginia-law/virginia-property-and-real-estate-laws.html

What are the basic principles of value in real estate? (2019, January 15). High Rockies Living. https://www.highrockiesliving.com/basic-principles-of-value-explained/

What are the factors that affect the real estate market? (n.d.). Blox. https://blox.xyz/blog/what-are-the-factors-that-affect-the-real-estate-market

What are the most effective ways to delegate tasks in real estate? (n.d.). Linkedin. https://www.linkedin.com/advice/3/what-most-effective-ways-delegate-tasks-real-estate-mgvzc

What is cash flow and how it is calculated in real estate? (2023, January 16). TimesProperty. https://timesproperty.com/news/post/how-is-cashflow-calculated-in-real-estate-blid3680

What you should know about risk assessment and real estate. (2018, October 26). Oxford Companies. https://oxfordcompanies.com/blog/what-you-should-know-about-risk-assessment-and-real-estate/

Wieland, D. (2020, August 5). *Council post: Assessing three types of risk in real estate.* Forbes. https://www.forbes.com/sites/forbesrealestatecouncil/2020/08/05/assessing-three-types-of-risk-in-real-estate/?sh=38c3ed406a30

Wilson, N. (2023, October 17). *Tips for giving your real estate career a boost.* Opportunity Connection. https://opportunityconnection.net/effective-strategies-for-enhancing-real-estate-career/

Yadav, G. (2023, December 1). *The role of location in property valuation: What matters most?* Valocity Global. https://www.valocityglobal.com/en-in/2023/12/the-role-of-location-in-property-valuation-what-matters-most/

Your essential guide to navigating the home loan process. (2023, September 25). Keller Home Loans.

https://kwlends.com/your-essential-guide-to-navigating-the-home-loan-process/

Made in the USA
Monee, IL
04 November 2026

67380054R00075